All of the beverage recipes contained within can be prepared using a minimum number of ingredients and appliances. There are no blender drinks, no raw eggs, ice cream, vegetable juices, teas, or alcoholic beverages, as required ingredients.

Thus the home or professional user can prepare and enjoy these delicious beverages while adhering to the utmost in sober simplicity.

**The word *espresso* first appeared in American print in 1945.**

The word *cappuccino* first appeared
in American print in 1948.

# Acknowledgments

Special thanks to the hundreds of people without whose support and input this project would not have been possible.

To my sons Scott and Greg and my daughter Bunny for your valuable assistance and support in this project.

To my mother, my brothers and sisters, for excusing me from the family get-togethers in order to meet the writing and publishing deadlines.

Special thanks to Rich Abker, for without his numerous contributions and dedicated support, this work could not have been completed.

To Dennis Simon, Tim Matelich, Robin Krause, Kristin Connors, Bill Adams, Jerry Long, Paul Blauert, and Gary Laidler, for handling the production and business end of this project.

To Cherie Crowley and Thom Head for the illustrations and graphics.

To Mario Rosito, Michael Girgis, and Michael Teahan of Rosito Bisani importers for their technical input and allowing the use of the Brasilia espresso machine appearing on the cover.

To Jennifer Johnson, Mary Whittington and Linda Packard for your editing services.

To Ian Bersten, Ph.D., author of *Coffee Floats—Tea Sinks,* and to Dr. Ernesto Illy, two of the world's foremost espresso and coffee experts, who have answered many of my questions.

To Jim Glang, owner of Crossroads Espresso, one of my first and most knowledgeable teachers.

To Mauro Cipolla, owner of Caffé D'arté, one of Seattle's top gourmet roasters. I've lost count of the number of Coffee Academy sessions I have attended. Thank you, Mauro. You have been a great teacher. "Taste the difference."

To Bill Stearns, president of Stearns & Lehman Inc., makers of Dolce "Italian Style" syrups, for his help and encouragement of this work.

To Neal Cowan, author of *Sip of Seattle,* the first espresso coupon book ever.

To Craig Walters and Bob Perna, producers of *Gourmet Coffee,* great video for home espresso.

To Bruce Milletto and Ed Ardvison, producers of *Espresso 101,* winner of *Fresh Cup* magazine's 'Spressy award for the best overall espresso "how to" video, September 1994.

To Louis Nicolaides, author of *L.A. Caffé* and other regional coffeehouse guides.

To Dana Rafferty, Vice President of Saeco® USA Inc., for your expert advice on home espresso equipment.

To Michael and Becky McGraw of Bev Tech Inc.; Barbara Hausner of Melitta® North America Inc.; and Phil Campbell and Susie Cover of RSVP International, wholesale distributors, for your advice and continued support.

To Craig Kiggens of Espresso Gears, commercial espresso equipment repair service, for the knowledge you've imparted on troubleshooting espresso equipment.

To David Schomer, gourmet roaster, coffee trade writer, and retail operator. I've learned so much from you.

To the staffs and publishers of two outstanding national espresso trade publications: *Cafe Olé*—Seattle, WA, and *Fresh Cup*—Portland, OR. Your encouragement and assistance were invaluable.

To William "Fergy" Ferguson, writer of *How to Open Your Espresso Cart,* and Keri Goodman, cowriter of *Java "U" Business Basics,* both great manuals.

To Bob Burgess and Vic Belonis of Burgess Enterprises, pioneers of the Northwest espresso movement, for your valuable input.

To my friends Debi and Ken McAlpine, owners of Le Bistro Coffeehouse in Gig Harbor, WA, for your assistance.

To Craig Bunney, owner of Northstar, for your suggestions and advice.

To David Latimer and Kathleen McGee of "Coffee Works," *The Cafe Business Journal,* San Francisco, CA, for your network support.

To Ted Lingle, executive director of the Specialty Coffee Association of America, and to your wonderful organization, for all of the invaluable statistical data.

Special thanks for your recipes and other contributions: Bill Mohrweis, Dan Pietela, Todd Wilson, Cheryl and Larry Appel, Cindy Tripp, Dan Lundenberg, Matt Brandenburger of Torani Syrups, Dane Poulton of Stasero Syrups, Dale Nelson of Vitali Syrups, Doug Gerber of DaVinci™ Syrups, Alan Johnson and Lars-Erik Persson of Monin Syrups, Ali Vincent of Caravali Coffees, Joseph Staffieri of San Marino Syrups, Earl Greiner and Heidi Brown of Stirling Syrups, Rick Swanson of Oscar's Syrups, Marvin Allain, Steve, Sandy and Betty Peterson, Bruce Ewen, Steve and Sandy Hosch and their barista Christy, Doug and Wendy Koehly, Barbara Abker, Jeff Whitehead, Ron Smick, Bernie Dorsey, Gary Smith, David Baron, Matt Pearson, Leonard Rivero, and Josh and Robyn, baristas at Caffé D'arté.

To Sue Bowden, for your assistance and your mixology and equipment presentation skills.

And to all the many others, THANK YOU!

## About the Author

Phil Janssen draws from over 30 years experience to create *Espresso Quick Reference Guide.* As top producing representative for a leading commercial espresso equipment manufacturer, Janssen has sold, installed, and performed training on over one hundred commercial espresso operations in the Seattle area. He is a professional mixologist experienced in trend analysis and has published widely in beverage industry trade journals.

As a working professional in America's premier espresso marketplace, Janssen recognized the absence of an essential reference guide. Responding to repeated requests from his customers and professional colleagues, he devoted over 6,000 hours to creating a text intended primarily to serve that trade audience.

His first book, *Espresso Seattle Style Quick Reference Guide,* appeared in September 1993. In it Janssen prominently featured instruction on the preparation of Seattle-style beverages, and he included technical suggestions on the use and maintenance of professional espresso equipment. Trade response was immediate and profound: The first printing sold out in under two months, and as this new edition goes to press some 25,000 copies have been sold.

Heartened by the acceptance of the professional marketplace, Janssen has turned to the home espresso maker in this new and much expanded edition of his reference guide. Included are new recipes, new techniques, a survey of emerging trends, and thousands of snippets of trivia—all intended to make it easy and fun to practice the "inexact science" of espresso and Italian syrup beverages at home.

# Contents

# Introduction

Espresso and the gourmet coffee craze are sweeping the U.S. and spreading worldwide.

This specialty coffee renaissance was pioneered in Seattle, where gourmet coffee sales have reached a 40% market share, almost twice the current national average. This anomaly is largely explained by two factors: First, strong regional brands have emerged among custom coffee roasters. Second, a unique retail phenomenon has evolved in the Northwest, the espresso street vending cart. The first such cart appeared in 1978 beneath the Seattle monorail, and by 1994 over 450 carts were in operation in the metropolitan area alone.

Such is the current popularity of espresso in Seattle that businesses featuring it include hardware stores, car washes, salons, department stores, nurseries, hospitals, bike shops, and even one dentist whose marquee advertises "Espresso Dental."

A recent national survey showed that in the past decade there has been an increase in the U.S. by 28% of those abstaining from alcohol. The moderation trend of the '80s has opened the door for the booming gourmet coffee industry.

The soda fountains of the '50s have become the espresso bars of the '90s, complete with a wide array of hot and cold espresso based beverages and Italian style sodas.

*Espresso* quite literally means *fast coffee:* Water heated to 195°F is forced at 130 pounds of pressure through finely ground roasted coffee beans. Within 18 to 23 seconds, the process is complete. Highly concentrated flavor and aroma characterize the finished beverage and distinguish it from coffee produced by the common drip method.

In Italy where coffee and espresso are synonymous, over 90% of espresso is consumed straight. The inverse proportion is true in the U.S. where over 90% of all espresso beverages are diluted with milk in the form of lattes, mochas and cappuccinos.

The art of preparing espresso beverages is both fun and easy. We generally use only a limited number of ingredients: ground coffee, milk, and Italian style syrups. Quality home espresso machines and coffee grinders now make it possible for the homemaker to enjoy these same espresso creations that were only previously available at retail espresso bars.

In this reference guide we have attempted to remove much of the Italian terminology and to simplify the preparation technique so that the home user can master espresso, the social beverage of the '90s.

# Chapter 1

# Preface to the Recipes

Anyone can make coffee or espresso. In order to learn the art of making great coffee and great espresso, a serious understanding of coffee and extraction is necessary. This understanding is learned through education and training from those who have the knowledge.

*Espresso* means fast coffee: 130 pounds of pressurization allows the beverage to be extracted in 18-23 seconds compared to the 4- to 6-minute brewing cycle of drip ground coffee.

Other distinctions between espresso and coffee are:
1. Espresso is brewed from a more flavorful gourmet bean than the commercial Robusta bean.
2. The Arabica bean contains approximately half the caffeine of the Robusta bean.
3. The espresso bean is generally roasted slightly longer for a darker roast.
4. Beans used for espresso are ground to a finer consistency just prior to brewing.
5. Espresso is brewed one cup at a time as opposed to batch brewing.
6. In the U.S. most espresso drinks are combined with steamed milk; in Europe sugar is generally added to straight espresso.

Worldwide, 11 billion pounds of coffee change hands each year. Of that imported each year into the United States, gourmet specialty coffee sales have increased fivefold in the past ten years.

Over 60% of gourmet coffee purchasers in the U.S. are women.

With more than 50% of the U.S. adult population drinking coffee at a rate of 3.58 cups per day in 1993, consumption was the highest in the past seven years.

Why have gourmet coffee and espresso become the social beverages of the 90s? Is it because in the past 10 years, the teetotaler count is up by 28% in the U.S.? We're drinking mochas, not martinis. . . .

The Specialty Coffee Association of America projects that by the year 1999, some 10,000 coffee cafes, espresso bars, and carts will be in operation in the U.S.

In 1993, U.S. consumers purchased 88% of coffee of the ground variety for home use. Whole bean coffee comprised only 12%, but this variety is projected to grow at the rate of 20% per year.

"Home" was the preferred location for consuming coffee in the U.S. in 1993. Seventy percent of all coffee was consumed there.

Seattle has become the espresso capital of the world with gourmet coffee sales reaching 40% of the total coffee market share. The national average is about 30%.

In the June 26, 1994, edition of a major Seattle daily, it was reported that the Seattle area was the home of 450 espresso carts, 4,000 commercial espresso machines, and as many as 10,000 baristas (espresso bartenders).

The Specialty Coffee Association of America (SCAA) is based in Long Beach, CA. In the three-year period from July 1991 to July 1994, membership increased from 356 to 1,822 members.

Ninety percent of espresso in Italy is consumed straight, the other 10% is taken cappuccino style with foamed and steamed milk. The name *cappuccino* is said to have derived from either the chocolate color of Capuchin monks' robes or from the curl of their hoods, which is duplicated in foamed milk on the top of a perfect cappuccino.

A barista is a title given to one who has mastered the art of making espresso beverages.

In the U.S., 90% of espresso beverages are served with steamed and/or foamed milk.

Milk contains lactose (milk sugar) and casein which diminish the bitterness in coffee. The popularity of milk based espresso beverages can be attributed to this marriage.

The latte made with foamed/steamed milk is the most called-for espresso beverage in the U.S. The actual word is derived from the Italian *Caffè Latte*.

*Latte* is the Italian word for milk. If you request a latte in Italy, you will be served a glass of milk.

In Italy the most common coffee beverages are straight espresso with sugar, espresso with a dollop of milk foam called an espresso macchiato, and cappuccino. Cappuccinos are commonly served in a small bowl at breakfast.

A taste romance ensues when hot milk is married with gourmet coffee. Heating by steaming actually alters the proteins and sugars of milk. The process creates a pleasantly different taste that blends well with espresso.

In the Puget Sound area of Washington, the popularity of whole bean coffee is such that a local dairy has begun delivering coffee beans to home route customers along with fresh milk.

The espresso machine was invented in France but was perfected and first manufactured in Italy at the turn of the 20th century.

Gourmet coffee roasters in the U.S. use the high grade Arabica beans almost exclusively.

 An espresso blend is made by mixing two or more straight Arabica bean varieties to improve its flavor, aroma, or taste attributes.

 Approximately 2,000 coffee cherries yield about one pound of coffee beans.

 Each cherry contains two coffee beans. Approximately 60 of these beans produce a shot of espresso made with seven grams of ground coffee.

 The art of espresso mixology is fun and creative. Chances are if you ordered a mocha at ten separate retail locations, the mocha would be prepared at least four separate ways.

 A mocha is a chocolate latte, usually topped with whipped cream and chocolate garnish.

 A mocha can be made with any type of chocolate: thick chocolate syrup, thin chocolate syrup, sweet powdered chocolate, or chocolate milk.

 In 1905 Milton Hershey began mass-producing chocolate bars. Hershey, Pennsylvania, was named after him. Today his syrup in the plastic squeeze bottles is popular for flavoring our mochas.

Seattle has become the espresso and gourmet coffee hub of the world. This is due largely to the consumer awareness created by the city's major coffee roasters.

---

Heavy-bodied roasts are generally better for coffee beverages made with milk, such as lattes or cappuccinos.

---

The order for pouring ingredients into a serving cup for hot espresso specialty beverages is:
(1) Flavoring (optional)
(2) Espresso
(3) Steamed and foamed milk.

---

To prevent curdling of certain flavored syrups in espresso beverages, always add the syrups first, and don't steam the milk too hot. High acid content flavors are the worst culprits.

---

Syrups and sugar sweeteners are best dissolved if poured into the cup before the espresso or at least before the steamed milk.

---

Heat intensifies the sweetness of sugar. Thus, ¾ to 1 ounce of Italian flavored syrup is recommended to sweeten and flavor a 12-ounce hot espresso based beverage, and for a 16-ounce cold beverage filled ⅔ with ice, a 2-ounce portion of syrup would be recommended.

A professional barista is not only skilled in the preparation of espresso beverages, but is also a theatrical performer whose show includes: the sights, sounds, and aroma of grinding fresh beans; the sight and sounds of steaming milk; the portioning (dosing) and packing of ground coffee in the brew basket; the sight and aroma of extracting the espresso brew; and the mixing and garnishing of these ingredients.

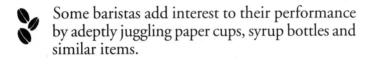

Some baristas add interest to their performance by adeptly juggling paper cups, syrup bottles and similar items.

In the heart of downtown Seattle (the site of the U.S.'s first espresso vending cart) the best in "live theater" can be witnessed at the break of dawn as the many baristas compete to outperform each other to boost their espresso sales.

The audio, visual, and aromatic aspects of creating each drink enhance the enjoyment of each espresso beverage.

Why do we say "coffee beans" when coffee comes from berries? Because each berry has two beans.

One pound of ground espresso beans will yield approximately 50 single shot servings, while the same amount of ground commercial coffee beans yields roughly 45 8-ounce servings.

## Major Contributor

Rich Abker, operations manager for Caffé D'arté in Seattle, Washington, has developed and perfected many techniques for making flavored espresso beverages, as well as Italian soda beverages. Rich's unique method of separately flavoring the espresso and the milk for his Double Funn Cappuccinos, along with his other flavoring and mixology techniques, have truly captured the "Seattle Style" theme.

The following are some of his useful methods for creating signature drinks from basic espresso beverages.

### Rich's Espresso Royales

#### Americano Royale
—Pour flavored syrup into serving cup.
—Fill ¾ way with hot water.
—Pour double shot of espresso into hot water.
—Top with whipped cream.
—Use flavored syrup to decorate whipped cream or garnish with toasted almonds, shredded coconut, grated maraschino cherries, etc.

#### Latte Royale
—Prepare a latte with no foam.
—Use flavor if desired.
—Add flavored whipped cream.

Latte Royales are two-flavored lattes that use only one syrup in the milk. The flavored whipped cream adds an enjoyable and interesting contrast.

### Rich's Fun Cappuccinos
—Use the same preparation technique applied in Rich's favorite cappuccino, except use flavored syrups of your choice.
—Pour one ounce of flavored syrup into milk to be steamed and frothed with dense foam cappuccino style (ex. vanilla).
—Garnish dense foam with a thick, flavored syrup or a mix of syrup and honey.
—Use pinched cup and pour thin strings of syrup over dense foam. (See illustration of pinched cup technique on page 22.)

### Rich's Double Funn Cappuccinos
The "Double Funn" is a two-flavor, two-color cappuccino that is enjoyable beyond expectations. The techniques used in making these creative espresso drinks are simple and easy.

—Pour ¼ oz of the dominant of the two syrup flavors into the serving cup (ex. chocolate).
—Pour about 1 oz of the mildest flavored syrup directly into the milk to be steamed and frothed (ex. vanilla).
—Pour ristretto espresso into the cup with flavored syrup; stir espresso when any *thick* syrup is used.
—Fill serving cup ¾ full with steamed flavored milk.
—Top with flavored dense foam two to three inches high until it forms a pointed cap.
—Garnish with a heavy flavored syrup. Use a pinched paper cup to apply thin strings of syrup in a decorative fashion. (See Rich's Funn Cappuccino examples.)

**Examples of flavored syrups to be used in Rich's Double Funn Cappuccinos:**

1. Strongest flavors into cup.
2. Mild flavored syrups into milk become dense foam and steamed milk.

Popular syrup flavors and examples of how they can be used. (Use your own creativity and other flavors.)

**1.  Flavors into cup:**

| | |
|---|---|
| Blackberry | Cranberry |
| Blueberry | Grape |
| Boysenberry | Irish Cream |
| Butterscotch | Kahlua |
| Cherry | Lemon |
| Chocolate | Lime |
| Chocolate Mint | Orange |
| Coffee | Pineapple |
| Creme de Cacao | Raspberry |
| Creme de Menthe | Strawberry |

**2.  Flavors into milk:**

| | |
|---|---|
| Almond | Hazelnut |
| Amaretto | Honey |
| Apricot | Peach |
| Apple | Praline |
| Banana | Rum |
| Cinnamon | Vanilla |
| Coconut | |

# HOW TO PREPARE RICH'S DOUBLE FUNN CAPPUCCINOS

**2.** Pour ½ ounce of dominant flavor—example: Chocolate—into serving cup.

**3.** Add espresso to flavor and stir.

**1.** Add ½ ounce flavored syrup—example: Vanilla—to cold milk, then foam and steam.

**4.** Pour flavored foamed/steamed milk over flavored espresso.

# RICH'S DOUBLE FUNN CAPPUCCINOS & LATTE ROYALES

Milk is flavored before it is foamed and steamed.

Flavored whipped cream topping

Chocolate syrup

Crushed nuts

Flavored foamed milk

Flavored steamed milk

Espresso

**LATTE ROYALE**

One flavor goes in the milk. The second goes into the serving cup.

**DOUBLE FUNN CAPPUCCINOS**

**Examples of Rich's Double Funn Cappuccino Recipes**
*(Use your imagination and pinched cup technique for designs.)*

1) Toasted Marshmallow
   —Irish cream into cup
   —Caramel (thin) into milk
   —Prepare cappuccino (See page 9)
   —Garnish with thick caramel syrup

2) Candy Apple Red
   —Cherry syrup into cup
   —Apple syrup into milk
   —Prepare cappuccino
   —Garnish with mixture of honey and cherry
      flavored syrup

3) Chocolate Wafer
   —Chocolate syrup into cup
   —Vanilla syrup into milk
   —Prepare cappuccino
   —Garnish with heavy chocolate syrup

4) Rum Runn
   —Use either butterscotch or praline in cup
   —Rum syrup into milk
   —Prepare cappuccino
   —Garnish with honey/rum syrup mixture

5) Coffee Nudge
   —Kahlua or coffee syrup into cup
   —Creme de cacao syrup into milk
   —Prepare cappuccino
   —Garnish dense foam with honey mixed with
      coffee syrup

6) Chocolate Covered Cherry
   —Chocolate syrup into cup
   —Cherry syrup into milk
   —Prepare cappuccino
   —Garnish dense foam with thick chocolate
      syrup

### Rich's Re-Macchiatos

—Pour ¼ ounce of your favorite syrup or
  combination of syrups into small serving cup.
—Pour double shot of ristretto espresso into cup
  and stir. (See ristretto on page 239.)
—Top with approximately two tablespoons dense
  foamed milk or whipped cream. Stir and serve.

Any single flavor syrup of your choice may be used.
However, there are many two-flavored combinations that
are excitingly good.


### Examples of Suggested Combinations of Flavored Syrups

Almond/Honey
Cherry/Almond
Cherry/Coconut
Cherry/Vanilla
Chocolate/Almond
Chocolate/Banana
Chocolate/Cherry
Chocolate/Coconut
Chocolate/Praline
Chocolate/Rum
Cinnamon/Honey
Irish Cream/Almond
Irish Cream/Kahlua
Lemon/Honey
Orange/Chocolate
Orange/Vanilla

# Rich's Favorite Espresso Techniques

A. **Straight Espresso**
   1. Ristretto: short pour (1 ounce single, 2 ounce double)
   2. Lungo: long pour (1½ ounce single, 3 ounce double)

B. **Americano**
   —Fill either 8 ounce or 12 ounce double cup ⅔ full with hot water. (Use a double cup to protect hands.)
   —Pull a double shot of ristretto espresso and pour into hot water. (Dense crema should float on top.)
   —Leave room for cream or sweetener if desired. Serve.

C. **The Perfect Latte**
   —See description on page 236.

D. **The Perfect Cappuccino**
   —See description on page 238.

E. **The Perfect Mocha**
   —Pour thick chocolate syrup into serving cup. (Add a few drops of caramel if you like.)
   —Pull a double shot of ristretto.
   —Begin steaming and frothing fresh cold milk while the espresso is pouring.
   —Prepare milk as you would for *The Perfect Latte,* page 236.
   —Pour espresso over chocolate and stir.
   —Pour in steamed/frothed milk.
   —Whipped cream is optional, so leave room if you choose to use it.
   —Garnish with thick chocolate syrup. (Use pinched cup method.)

**F. Brevé**

A brevé is any milk based espresso drink where half-and-half is substituted for milk. Brevés can be flavored or not.

—If flavored, pour flavored syrup into cup.

—Pull a double shot of ristretto.

—Steam and froth half-and-half as for a latte.

—Pour espresso into serving cup.

—Pour steamed and frothed milk into espresso. Serve. Garnish may be used.

—Brevé lattes and brevé mochas are popular.

**G. Iced Americano**

—Fill 16 ounce clear cup with crushed or small cubed ice ¾ full.

—Fill with cold water ¾ full.

—Pull a double shot of ristretto espresso and pour into cup. Add cream, sweetener, or flavored syrup. Stir and serve.

**H. Iced Latte/Brevé**

—Fill 16 ounce clear cup with crushed or small cubed ice ¾ full.

—Fill cup with cold milk or half-and-half ¾ full.

—Pull a double shot of ristretto espresso and pour into cup.

—Garnish with golf ball-sized whipped cream and large colored straw. Serve.

**I. Iced Mocha**

—Fill 16 ounce clear cup ¾ full with crushed or small cubed ice.

—Fill cup with fresh cold milk.

—Pour 2 ounces chocolate in pouring glass.

—Pull espresso directly over chocolate. Stir.

—Pour chocolate espresso into milk.

—Garnish with golf ball-sized whipped cream. Add a few drops of chocolate onto whipped cream. Use large colored straw. Serve.

## Rich's Favorite Italian Soda Techniques

**A.  Iced Italian Soda (single flavor)**
—Fill 16 ounce clear cup ¾ full with crushed or small cubed ice.
—Fill cup ¾ full with either soda, seltzer, or mineral water.
—Pour in 2 ounces of your favorite flavored syrup. To make this an Italian Cream Soda, sometimes called a Cremosa, simply float in two tablespoons of half-and-half.
—Garnish with a golf ball-sized whipped cream with a few drops of flavored syrup on the whipped cream. Use a large colored straw. Serve.

**B.  Rich's Italian Dream Sodas (two flavored syrups)**
—Fill 16 ounce clear cup ¾ full with crushed or small cubed ice.
—Pour in one ounce of the lightest of the two flavored syrups (vanilla, lemon, coconut).
—Fill cup ¾ full with either soda, seltzer, or mineral water.
—Pour in one ounce of the most colorful syrup (orange, cherry).
—Float 2 tablespoons of half-and-half.
—Garnish as usual for Italian Sodas.
—Serve and enjoy.

A tall latte (12 ounce cup) made with whole milk contains approximately 133 calories; with nonfat milk, 77 calories.

---

Each ounce of flavored syrup contains only about 100 calories.

---

A teaspoon of cane sugar contains about 18 calories.

---

Club soda has zero calories per ounce. Colas have 12 calories per ounce, and natural fruit juices have between 10 and 20 calories per ounce.

---

The popularity of iced coffee drinks has been attributed to the French colonial troops in North Africa, who took up drinking the chilled beverages to "beat the heat."

---

Phyllis Jordan, whose retail coffee stores are located in New Orleans, sells far more iced coffee than hot coffee. She has developed a cold-water steeping method to reduce the acids in the chilled product.

---

For their iced coffee, the Japanese prefer darker roasted beans. Most iced coffee served in Japan is served with sugar syrup and cream.

---

Pioneer Square in Seattle, Washington is reputed to have been the first location to serve iced lattes. The year—1978.

Just as tart lemonade is a better thirst quencher than sweet lemonade, diet drinks are better than sugary ones. Alcohol dehydrates you as well, increasing your thirst. Nonalcoholic Italian sodas and coffee beverages are better thirst quenchers.

The word *granita* is derived from the Italian words *gran* which means granular ice, and *ita* from the Italian *bibita*, which means soft drink, therefore, a granular ice drink.

Granita was introduced in Paris in 1660.

Such is the popularity of espresso in Seattle that businesses featuring it include hardware stores, car washes, salons, department stores, nurseries, hospitals, bike shops, and even one dentist whose marquee advertises "Espresso Dental."

Lemon or orangeade ice cubes add zest to any Italian soda beverage and will not dilute the drink as they melt.

For iced coffee recipes, brewing fresh coffee and then pouring it into ice cube trays will provide you with ice cubes that won't water down as they melt. Make the cubes of frozen milk or of real fruit juices for a variation on this theme.

Simple syrup (water and sugar) is much better for sweetening cold drinks than granulated sugar alone, which doesn't dissolve easily.

One Washington State espresso cart operator, due to limited refrigerator storage, handles only two milks—2% and half-and-half. When customers request that their lattes be made with whole milk, he mixes the two.

If you stir sweetened, condensed milk into your steeping black coffee, you are following Vietnamese tradition that goes back to colonial times.

One homemade ice cube, when melted, makes about one ounce of water.

For crystal clear ice cubes pour hot rather than cold water into the trays.

A svizzle was a rum-based beverage served in the Caribbean and the West Indies. The stir sticks were named after the drink.

One soda fountain in Dallas is reportedly doing a brisk business selling "Jr. Rum and Cokes" with nonalcoholic Italian style rum-flavored syrup.

Remember: do not stir soda or carbonated based beverages vigorously, or they lose their sparkle.

Cherry-flavored and colored toothpicks with a fruit garnish add a special touch to iced Italian beverages.

In ancient Sicily, disputes over water rights to the olive groves often left some growing regions dry. Drinking vessels were sanitized by wiping the inside with lemon rind.

The very first coffee cart? The year was 1672: an Armenian served coffee from a kiosk at the St. Germane Fair in Paris. Business was good. Soon he sent young men door-to-door with coffee in urns heated by charcoal braziers or lamps.

Provide a candy cane as a stir stick for your vanilla lattes during the Christmas season.

A frosty and very classy sugar rim on your cold drink glass can be achieved by having two saucers—one with a dampened towel and the other with ¼ inch of sugar. Dampen the rim of the glass on the towel, then dip it in the sugar.

For flavored whipped cream, add four ounces of flavored syrup to one pint of whipping cream and beat in a chilled container.

Real whipped cream topping will hold its surface much better than canned whipped cream, which is too light and will rapidly wilt at room temperature.

For cappuccinos, decorate the white head of foam with garnishes of powdered chocolate, nutmeg, cinnamon, or colored sprinkles.

# DECORATIONS

PINCHED CUP
TECHNIQUE

Create your own designs
by pouring thick flavored
syrups from a pinched
paper cup.

Examples of flavors:
-Chocolate
-Honey
-Caramel
-Maple Syrup
-Flavored Honey

One Northwest caterer, whose clients are among the well-to-do, serves flaming lattes at the end of meals. He ignites fruit flavored extracts containing 80% alcohol and dusts this flame with ground cinnamon, creating sparks. Use caution when trying this technique.

---

 Only the unique interaction of certain flavors creates the symphonies of taste in multi-flavored syrup recipes.

---

 The key word is *passion*; all successful industry people share this passion for coffee.

# FIVE BASIC
# ESPRESSO DRINKS

ESPRESSO

Whipped cream

Crema

MOCHA

CAPPUCCINO

AMERICANO

Shot of espresso poured on top of hot water

Brown and white marble swirl

Marbleized with espresso and dense foamed and steamed milk.

Espresso

Foamed milk
Steamed milk

LATTE

*Heavy-bodied roasts are generally better for coffee beverages made with milk, such as lattes or cappuccinos.

# Chapter 2

# Recipes

## BASIC ESPRESSO AND ICED ITALIAN STYLE BEVERAGES

### Americano

A gourmet cup of coffee, made by pouring one or two shots of espresso over a 6 oz cup of hot water. The crema from the espresso will float on top.

### Brevé

Any milk based espresso beverage where half-and-half is substituted for milk. Brevés can be flavored.

### Cappuccino

An espresso based beverage, topped with equal parts of steamed and foamed milk (wet cappuccino). A dry cappuccino is topped with all foamed milk. The milk is foamed/steamed prior to the espresso extraction, allowing the foam to set, or jell. The foam topping is shaped to form a peak (cap) on the cappuccino. Cappuccinos are usually dusted with nutmeg, cinnamon, or chocolate powder.

### Doppio

Double shot of espresso with one shot of water.

### Espresso

Properly done, espresso is made from a special blend of Arabica coffees, chosen for intense aromatic flavors and quality of performance during extraction. Espresso uses freshly roasted beans that are finely ground in the correct amount, firmly packed and then extracted under pressure. The end result will be a rich concentration of coffee taste and aroma, topped with a dense golden-brown foam called crema.

### Espresso Con Panna

An espresso serving topped with a dollop of whipped cream.

### Espresso Romano

A serving of straight espresso, with a twist of lemon added.

### Iced Espresso based Beverages

Are served in clear plastic or clear glassware. If flavored, the flavoring is added first, then the espresso. Stirred if thick syrup is used. Ice is then added. Cup is filled with *cold milk*. Can be topped with whipped cream.

### Italian Soda

An iced beverage usually served in a 14-16 oz clear plastic cup, flavored by 2 oz of Italian style syrup or syrups (usually fruit-based) and filled to the top with soda water. The recommended mix ratio is one part syrup to four parts soda water. Italian sodas can be topped with whipped cream.

### Italian Cream Soda (Cremosa)

Same as the Italian soda, but the soda water pour is stopped ½" from the top of the cup, and the beverage is filled with approximately 2 oz of half-and-half. Italian cream sodas can be topped with whipped cream.

A variation in the order of ingredients for Italian cream sodas: after pouring the flavors first, add the half-and-half second and the soda water last. A successful cart operator claims this approach is his key to increased sales.

### Latte

An espresso based beverage, where a very dense mixture of foamed/steamed milk at 140°F is poured down the side of a cup containing a serving of espresso. The pour allows the milk and espresso to marbleize, forming a very dense mixture. The taste of the espresso can be experienced with the first sip.

For a flavored latte in:

| | |
|---|---|
| 8 oz cup | add ½ oz flavoring |
| 12 oz cup | add ¾ oz flavoring |
| 16 oz cup | add 1 oz flavoring |

### Latteccino

An espresso based beverage with two parts steamed milk and one part foamed milk (a cross between a cappuccino and a latte).

### Lungo

This is the Italian word for *long* and refers to a long pour of espresso. This extraction usually takes about 25 to 30 seconds and is primarily for straight shots, using 1½ to 2 ounces of hot water for extracting the correct amount of coffee in a single portion.

### Macchiato

The Italian word for *marked.* There are two types of macchiatos: 1) straight espresso marked with a dollop of warm milk froth and 2) a steamed milk macchiato (latte or cappuccino) where the steamed milk is marked with an espresso poured slowly over the milk foam at the side of a clear glass. This will display a layered effect and is used in restaurants.

### Mocha

A chocolate flavored latte with an option of whipped cream for garnish and enjoyment.

### Ristretto

Ristretto means *restricted* in Italian. It is a short pour of espresso (highly concentrated) using ¾ to 1 ounce of hot water for extracting the correct amount of coffee in a double or single portion.

### Steamer

A serving of foamed/steamed milk, which has been flavored with 1 oz of Italian style syrup. Usually topped with whipped cream. *No espresso.* (Same as hot chocolate, but using Italian style syrup to flavor the milk).

Cup sizes used for the following recipes unless otherwise noted are:

 Hot drinks
12 oz

 Cold drinks
16 oz

Simple rule for order of the ingredients in both hot and cold drinks:
First—Flavor
Second—Espresso
Third—Milk or beverage used
Fourth—Garnish

Cup Sizes:
8 oz—Short
12 oz—Tall
16 oz—Grandé

Thin Italian style syrups will mix with the espresso without stirring.

Thick syrups such as Hershey's chocolate should be stirred *after* adding the espresso.

Purists generally agree to a 1 oz to 1¼ oz single shot portion of espresso. Some commercial operations even pour a double shot standard in all their drinks. In the majority of the following recipes, the espresso shot size will not be specified. We will just say "Pour Espresso," and let you determine your own shot size portion.

# A

###  ACE OF CLUBS SODA

Over Ice, Pour ⅔ oz each Syrup: Creme de Cassis, Lemon, Peppermint. Fill with Soda Water.

###  AFTER SUPPER COOLER

Over Ice, Pour ⅔ oz each Syrup: Apricot, Lemon, Mango. Fill with Soda Water.

###  ALABAMA SLAMMER

Over Ice, Pour 1 oz each Syrup: Amaretto, Peach. Fill with Soda Water.

###  ALBEMARLE FIZZ

Over Ice, Pour ½ oz Lemon Syrup, 1½ oz Raspberry Syrup. Fill with Soda Water.

###  ALEXANDER

Pour 2 oz Creme de Cacao Syrup. Add Espresso. Add Ice. Fill with Half-and-Half. Top with Whipped Cream.

###  ALMOND ICED COFFEE

Pour 1½ oz Almond Syrup, ½ oz Vanilla Syrup. Add Espresso. Add Ice. Fill with Cold Milk.

###  ALMOND JOY

Pour ¼ oz each Syrup: Chocolate, Coconut, Almond. Add Espresso. Fill with Foamed/Steamed Milk. Top with Whipped Cream.

### ALMOND LATTE

Pour ¾ oz Almond Syrup. Add Espresso. Fill with Foamed/Steamed Milk.

### ALMOND MIST STEAMER

Pour 1 oz Almond Syrup. Fill with Foamed/Steamed Milk and top with Whipped Cream.

# A

### ALMOND MOCHA
Pour ¾ oz Thick Chocolate Syrup, ½ oz Almond Syrup. Add Espresso. Stir. Fill with Foamed/Steamed Milk. Top with Whipped Cream and Chocolate Sprinkles.

### ALMOND MOCHA CREAM SODA
Over Ice, Pour 1 oz each Syrup: Almond, Chocolate. Add 3 oz Soda Water. Fill with Half-and-Half. Top with Whipped Cream. Dust with Chocolate Powder.

### ALMOND MOCHA ITALIAN SODA
Over Ice, Pour 1 oz each Syrup: Almond, Creme de Cacao. Fill with Soda Water.

### ALMOND MOCHA STEAMER
Pour ½ oz each Syrup: Almond, Chocolate. Fill with Foamed/Steamed Milk. Top with Whipped Cream. Dust with Chocolate Powder.

### ALMOND MOO
Pour ¾ oz Almond Syrup. Add Espresso. Fill with Foamed/Steamed Milk. Top with Whipped Cream and Chocolate Sprinkles.

### ALMOND ROCA MOCHA
Pour ½ oz each Thick Syrup: Chocolate, Butterscotch. Add ¼ oz Almond Syrup. Add Espresso. Stir. Fill with Foamed/Steamed Milk. Top with Whipped Cream and Chocolate Sprinkles.

# A

**AMALFIS**
Over Ice, Pour 2 oz any Flavored Syrup. Fill with Soda Water to ½" from top of cup. Stir. Top with Heavy Cream.

**AMARETTO & CREAM SODA**
Over Ice, Pour 2 oz Amaretto Syrup. Add Soda Water to ½" from top of cup. Top with Half-and-Half.

**AMARETTO COFFEE**
Pour ¾ oz Amaretto Syrup and 5 oz Hot Water. Add Espresso.

**AMARETTO EGG NOG LATTE**
Pour ¾ oz Amaretto Syrup. Add Espresso. Fill with Foamed/Steamed Egg Nog. Top with Whipped Cream. Dust with Nutmeg.

**AMARETTO MIST**
Over Ice, Pour 1½ oz Amaretto Syrup, ½ oz Lemon Syrup. Fill with Soda Water.

**AMARETTO ORANGE ITALIAN SODA**
Over Ice, Pour 1 oz each Syrup: Amaretto, Orange. Fill with Soda Water.

**AMARETTO ROSE**
Over Ice, Pour 1½ oz Amaretto Syrup, ½ oz Lime Syrup. Fill with Soda Water.

**AMARETTO STRAWBERRY LATTE**
Pour ½ oz each Syrup: Amaretto, Strawberry. Add Espresso. Fill with Foamed/Steamed Milk.

**AMARETTO SOUR COOLER**
Over Ice, Pour 1⅓ oz Amaretto Syrup, ⅔ oz Lemon Syrup. Fill with Soda Water.

# A

## AMARETTO SOUR LATTE

Pour ½ oz Amaretto Syrup, ¼ oz Lemon Syrup. Add Espresso. Fill with Foamed/Steamed Milk.

## AMARETTO STINGER

Over Ice, Pour 1½ oz Amaretto Syrup, ½ oz Creme de Menthe Syrup. Fill with Soda Water.

## AMBASSADOR'S MORNING LIFT

Pour ¾ oz Creme de Cacao Syrup. Add Espresso. Fill with Foamed/Steamed Egg Nog.

## AMERICANO

Pour 6 oz Hot Water. Top with Espresso.

## ANGEL FACE

Over Ice, Pour 1 oz each Syrup: Apricot, Apple. Fill with Soda Water.

## ANGEL'S MIST

Over Ice, Pour 1 oz each Syrup: Orange, Pineapple. Add Soda Water to ½" from top. Fill with Half-and-Half and splash with Lime Syrup.

## ANGEL'S TOUCH

Over Ice, Pour 1 oz each Syrup: Creme de Cacao, Creme de Cassis. Fill with Half-and-Half.

## ANGEL'S TOUCH 2

Over Ice, Pour 1 oz each Syrup: Creme de Cassis, Vanilla. Add 3 oz Soda Water. Fill with Half-and-Half.

## APPLE & SPICE SPRITZER

Over Ice, Pour 1½ oz Apple Syrup, ½ oz Cinnamon Syrup. Fill with Soda Water. Splash with Lime Syrup.

# A

### APPLE CIDER
Splash each Syrup in cup: Cinnamon, Lemon. Fill with Steamed Apple Cider. Dust with Nutmeg. Add 2 Cinnamon Sticks.

### APPLE COFFEE
Pour ½ oz Apple Syrup, ¼ oz Praline Syrup. Add 4 oz Hot Water and Espresso. Top with Cinnamon Stick.

### APPLE COLADA
Over Ice, Pour ⅔ oz each Syrup: Apple, Coconut. Add Soda Water to ½" from top of cup. Top with 2 oz Half-and-Half.

### APPLE PIE
Over Ice, Pour ¼ oz each Syrup: Cinnamon, Amaretto. Add 1½ oz Apple Syrup. Fill with Soda Water to ¼" from top of cup. Top with Whipped Cream.

### APPLE RUM DUM COOLER
Over Ice, Pour ¾ oz each Syrup: Apple, Rum. Add ¼ oz each Syrup: Almond, Lime. Fill with Soda Water.

### APPLE SOUR COOLER
Over Ice, Pour 1½ oz Apple Syrup. Add ½ oz Lemon Syrup. Fill with Soda Water. Splash with Lemon Syrup.

### APPLE SPARKLE
Over Ice, Pour 1¾ oz Apple Syrup, ¼ oz Lemon Syrup. Fill with Soda Water.

### APPLE TODDY
Steam 8 oz Apple Juice. Pour into cup. Add ½ teaspoon Brown Sugar. Stir. Sprinkle with Cinnamon.

# A

 **APPLE WALDORF BREVÉ**

Pour ½ oz Apple Syrup, ¼ oz each Syrup: Cinnamon, Hazelnut. Add Espresso. Fill with Foamed/Steamed Half-and-Half and top with Whipped Cream. Dust with Cinnamon Powder or Nutmeg Powder.

 **APPLEJACK**

Over Ice, Pour 1½ oz Apple Syrup, ½ oz Lemon Syrup. Fill with Soda Water.

**APPLEJACK PUNCH**

Over Ice, Pour 1½ oz Apple Syrup, ½ oz Orange Syrup. Fill with Soda Water. Splash with Grenadine Syrup.

**APPLESAUCE LATTE**

Pour ½ oz Apple Syrup, splash of Cinnamon Syrup. Add ½ teaspoon Brown Sugar. Add Espresso. Stir. Fill with Foamed/Steamed Milk. Dust with Cinnamon Powder.

 **APRES TENNIS BRACER**

Over Ice, Pour ½ oz Orange Syrup. Fill with Ginger Ale.

 **APRICOT ALMOND SPICED SODA**

Over Ice, Pour ⅔ oz each Syrup: Apricot, Almond. Add ¼ oz each Syrup: Lemon, Cinnamon. Fill with Soda Water.

 **APRICOT COOLER**

Over Ice, Pour 2 oz Apricot Syrup. Fill with Soda Water.

# A

 **APRICOT FIZZ**
Over Ice, Pour 1¾ oz Apricot Syrup, ¼ oz Lemon Syrup. Fill with Soda Water.

 **APRICOT LADY**
Over Ice, Pour 1¾ oz Apricot Syrup, ¼ oz Lime Syrup. Fill with Soda Water to ¼" from top of cup. Top with Half-and-Half.

 **APRICOT PIE SODA**
Over Ice, Pour 1½ oz Apricot Syrup. Add ¼ oz each Syrup: Cinnamon, Rum. Fill with Soda Water. Splash with Lemon Syrup.

 **ARIZONA SUNSHINE**
Pour a double shot Espresso. Add Ice. Add ¾ oz each Syrup: Rum, Vanilla. Fill with Cold Water. Stir.

 **ASIAN ICED COFFEE**
Pour 1 oz Pineapple Syrup. Add Espresso. Add Ice. Fill with Cold Water.

 **AZTEC GOLD SODA**
Over Ice, Pour ⅔ oz each Syrup: Passion Fruit, Mandarino, Almond. Fill with Soda Water.

 **BAHAMA MAMA 1**
Over Ice, Pour ⅔ oz each Syrup: Creme de Cacao, Coconut, Pineapple. Fill with Soda Water. Splash with Grenadine Syrup.

 **BAHAMA MAMA 2**
Over Ice, Pour ½ oz each Syrup: Coconut, Coffee, Pineapple, Rum. Fill with Soda Water. Top with a splash of Grenadine Syrup.

# B

 **BAHAMIAN COFFEE**

Pour ¾ oz Praline Syrup. Add Espresso. Fill with Steamed Milk. Add Cinnamon Stick.

 **BALI HAI SODA**

Over Ice, Pour ½ oz each Syrup: Rum, Lime, Almond, and Apple. Fill with Soda Water.

 **BALTIMORE BRACER**

Over Ice, Pour 1 oz each Syrup: Orange, Anisette. Fill with Soda Water.

 **BANANA BREAD LATTE**

Pour ⅜ oz each Syrup: Banana, Creme de Cacao. Add a splash of Cinnamon Syrup. Add Espresso. Fill with Foamed/Steamed Milk. Splash with Banana Syrup.

**BANANA CHERRY CREAM SODA**

Over Ice, Pour 1 oz each Syrup: Banana, Cherry. Add 3 oz Soda Water. Fill with Half-and-Half.

 **BANANA COCONUT LATTE**

Pour ½ oz each Syrup: Banana, Coconut. Add Espresso. Fill with Foamed/Steamed Milk.

**BANANA COFFEE CREAM SODA**

Over Ice, Pour 1 oz each Syrup: Banana, Coffee. Add Soda Water to ½" from top of cup. Fill with Half-and-Half.

 **BANANA COW**

Over Ice, Pour ½ oz Creme de Cacao Syrup, 1½ oz Banana Syrup. Fill with Milk. Splash with Banana Syrup.

# B

### ♨ BANANA CREAM BREVÉ

Pour ¾ oz Banana Syrup. Add Espresso. Fill with Foamed/ Steamed Half-and-Half. Top with Whipped Cream. Dust with Nutmeg.

### ♨ BANANA EGG NOG LATTE

Pour ¾ oz Banana Syrup. Add Espresso. Fill with Foamed/ Steamed Egg Nog. Dust with Nutmeg.

### ♨ BANANA GORILLA

Pour ¾ oz Thick Chocolate Syrup. Add ½ oz Banana Syrup. Add Espresso. Stir. Fill with Foamed/Steamed Milk. Top with Whipped Cream and Chocolate Sprinkles.

### BANANA MANGO CREAM SODA

Over Ice, Pour 1 oz each Syrup: Banana, Mango. Add Soda Water to ½" from top of cup. Top with Half-and-Half.

### ♨ BANANA MOO

Pour ¾ oz Banana Syrup. Add Espresso. Fill with Foamed/ Steamed Milk.

### BANANA NUT CREAM

Over Ice, Pour 1 oz each Syrup: Banana, Hazelnut. Add 3 oz Soda Water. Fill with Half-and-Half. Top with Whipped Cream.

### ♨ BANANA NUT LATTE

Pour ⅔ oz Banana Syrup, ¼ oz Hazelnut Syrup. Add Espresso. Fill with Foamed/ Steamed Milk.

### ♨ BANANA NUT TOFFEE LATTE

Pour ¼ oz each Syrup: Banana, Hazelnut, Caramel, Coffee. Add Espresso. Fill with Foamed/Steamed Milk.

**BANANA ORANGE CREAM SODA**

Over Ice, Pour 1 oz each Syrup: Banana, Orange. Add Soda Water to ½" from top of cup. Top with Half-and-Half.

 **BANANA RUM CREAM SODA**

Over Ice, Pour 1 oz each Syrup: Banana, Rum. Add Soda Water to ½" from top of cup. Top with Half-and-Half.

 **BANANA SPLIT**

Pour ⅓ oz each Syrup: Thick Chocolate, Banana, Strawberry. Add Espresso. Stir. Fill with Foamed/Steamed Milk. Top with Whipped Cream and Chocolate Sprinkles.

 **BANGER**

Over Ice, Pour 1 oz Orange Syrup, ¾ oz Almond Syrup, ½ oz Vanilla Syrup. Fill with Soda Water.

 **BANSHEE**

Over Ice, Pour 1½ oz Banana Syrup, ½ oz Creme de Cacao Syrup. Fill with Half-and-Half.

 **BAPTIST WINE**

Over Ice, Pour 1 oz Creme de Cassis Syrup. Add Soda Water to ½" from top of cup. Fill with Ginger Ale.

 **BARBERRY COAST CREAM COOLER**

Over Ice, Pour 1 oz each Syrup: Rum, Creme de Cacao. Add Soda Water to ½" from top of cup. Top with Half-and-Half.

 **BATIDA CARNIVAL**

Over Ice, Pour ⅓ oz each Syrup: Mango, Orange, Rum. Fill with Soda Water. Splash with Grenadine Syrup.

# B

 **BAVARIAN MINT LATTE**

Pour ½ oz each Syrup: Chocolate Mint, Coffee. Add Espresso. Fill with Foamed/ Steamed Milk.

 **BEACH BLANKET BINGO**

Over Ice, Pour 1 oz each Syrup: Cranberry, Grape. Fill with Soda Water. Splash with Lime Syrup.

**BEACHCOMBER**

Over Ice, Pour 1 oz Coconut Syrup, ½ oz Orange Syrup, ½ oz Lime Syrup. Fill with Soda Water. Splash with Grenadine Syrup.

 **BELGIAN BREVÉ**

Pour ½ oz Vanilla Syrup. Add Steamed Half-and-Half to ¾" from top and Foamed Half-and-Half to ¼" from top. Pour Espresso through the Half-and-Half, and top with Whipped Cream.

 **BELGIAN ORANGE COFFEE**

Pour ½ oz Orange Syrup. Add ¼ oz each Syrup: Cinnamon, Vanilla. Fill with Hot Water to ½" from top of cup. Top with Espresso. Dust with Cinnamon Powder.

 **BELIZ CREAM SODA**

Over Ice, Pour ⅔ oz each Syrup: Coconut, Coffee, Pineapple. Add Soda Water to ½" from top of cup. Fill with Half-and-Half. Splash with Cherry Syrup.

 **BELLEVUE SODA**

Over Ice, Pour ¾ oz Pineapple Syrup, ½ oz each Syrup: Coconut, Orange, Lime. Fill with Soda Water. Splash with Lime Syrup.

 **BELLINI**

Over Ice, Pour 1½ oz Peach Syrup, ½ oz Apple Syrup. Fill with Soda Water. Splash with Creme de Cassis Syrup.

# B

 **BELLINI SODA**
Over Ice, Pour 1⅓ oz Peach Syrup. Add ⅓ oz each Syrup: Apple, Grape. Fill with Soda Water. Splash with Lime Syrup.

 **BERMUDA BANQUET**
Over Ice, Pour 1 oz Apricot Syrup. Add ½ oz each Syrup: Lemon, Orange. Fill with Soda Water.

 **BERMUDA ROSE**
Over Ice, Pour 1½ oz Apricot Syrup, ½ oz Grenadine Syrup. Fill with Soda Water.

 **BIRD OF PARADISE**
Over Ice, Pour ½ oz each Syrup: Pineapple, Passion Fruit, Orange, Lemon. Fill with Soda Water. Splash with Grenadine Syrup.

 **BLACK & TAN**
Over Ice, Pour 5 oz Cola. Fill with Milk.

 **BLACK BELT SODA**
Over Ice, Pour 1½ oz Creme de Cassis Syrup, ½ oz Pineapple Syrup. Fill with Soda Water.

 **BLACK CARAMEL LATTE**
Pour ½ oz Caramel Syrup, ¼ oz Blackberry Syrup. Add Espresso. Fill with Foamed/ Steamed Milk.

 **BLACK CHERRY ITALIAN SODA**
Over Ice, Pour 1 oz each Syrup: Blackberry, Cherry. Add splash of Anisette Syrup. Fill with Soda Water.

 **BLACK CURRANT CREAM SODA**
Over Ice, Pour 2 oz Creme de Cassis Syrup. Add Soda Water to ½" from top of cup. Fill with Half-and-Half.

# B

 **BLACK FOREST MOCHA**

Pour 1 oz Thick Chocolate Syrup. Add ⅓ oz Cherry Syrup and Espresso. Stir. Fill with Foamed/Steamed Milk. Top with Whipped Cream. Dust with Chocolate Powder.

 **BLACK GRAPE COLA**

Over Ice, Pour Cola to ¼" from top of cup. Top with ½ oz Creme de Cassis Syrup.

 **BLACK LICORICE SODA**

Over Ice, Pour 1 oz each Syrup: Creme de Cacao, Licorice. Fill with Soda Water.

 **BLACK MAGIC**

Pour ¾ oz Coffee Syrup. Add Espresso. Fill with Foamed/ Steamed Milk. Splash with Lemon Syrup.

 **BLACK MARIA**

Pour ¾ oz Cherry Syrup. Add Espresso. Top with Foamed Milk and Chocolate Powder.

 **BLACK MARSHMALLOW SODA**

Over Ice, Pour ¾ oz Vanilla Syrup. Fill with Cola.

 **BLACK ORCHID**

Over Ice, Pour 1 oz Creme de Cassis Syrup. Add ½ oz each Syrup: Peach, Lemon. Fill with Soda Water.

 **BLACK PRINCE**

Over Ice, Pour 1¼ oz Blackberry Syrup, ¾ oz Chocolate Syrup. Fill with Soda Water.

 **BLACK RUSSIAN COLA**

Over Ice, Pour 1 oz Coffee Syrup, ½ oz Lime Syrup. Fill with equal parts Soda Water and Cola.

# B

## BLACKBERRY COCONUT LATTE

Pour ½ oz each Syrup: Blackberry, Coconut. Add Espresso. Fill with Foamed/Steamed Milk.

## BLACKBERRY RUM CREAM SODA

Over Ice, Pour 1 oz each Syrup: Blackberry, Rum. Add Soda Water to ½" from top of cup. Top with Half-and-Half.

## BLACKBERRY SUPREME COOLER 1

Over Ice, Pour 1 oz Blackberry Syrup, ½ oz Lemon Syrup. Add Soda Water to ½" from top of cup. Fill with Ginger Ale. Splash with Blackberry Syrup.

## BLACKBERRY SUPREME COOLER 2

Over Ice, Pour 1½ oz Blackberry Syrup, ½ oz Coconut Syrup. Fill with Soda Water. Splash with Lemon Syrup.

## BLUE MILK SPECIAL

A latte made with Nonfat Milk.

## BLUEBERRY CREAM BREVÉ

Pour ½ oz each Syrup: Blueberry, Vanilla. Add Espresso. Fill with Foamed/Steamed Half-and-Half.

## BLUEBERRY LEMON FIZZ

Over Ice, Pour 1⅓ oz Blueberry Syrup, ⅔ oz Lemon Syrup. Fill with Soda Water.

## BLUEBERRY RUM FIZZ

Over Ice, Pour 1 oz Blueberry Syrup, ¾ oz Rum Syrup, ¼ oz Lemon Syrup. Fill with Soda Water.

## BOCA CHICA COFFEE

Pour a double shot Espresso. Add Ice. Add 1 oz Rum Syrup, ½ oz Vanilla Syrup. Fill with Cold Water. Stir.

# B

 **BOCCIE BALL**
Over Ice, Pour 1¼ oz
of Amaretto Syrup,
¾ oz Orange Syrup.
Fill with Soda Water.

 **BOLERO COOLER**
Over Ice, Pour 1 oz
Rum Syrup, ½ oz each
Syrup: Apple, Lemon.
Fill with Soda Water.

 **BORA-BORA**
Over Ice, Pour ¾ oz
Pineapple Syrup, ½ oz
each Syrup: Passion
Fruit, Lemon, ¼ oz
Grenadine. Fill with
Soda Water. Splash
with Grenadine Syrup.

 **BORGIA**
Pour ¾ oz Creme de
Cacao Syrup. Add
Espresso. Top with
Whipped Cream. Dust
with Nutmeg.

 **BOSTON BANGER**
Over Ice, Pour 1 oz
Orange Syrup, ¾ oz
Almond Syrup, ½ oz
Vanilla Syrup. Fill with
Soda Water.

 **BOSTON COOLER**
Over Ice, Pour ½ oz
each Syrup: Lemon,
Grenadine. Add Soda
Water to ½" from top
of cup. Fill with Ginger
Ale.

 **BOSTON GOLD**
Over Ice, Pour 1½ oz
Orange Syrup, ½ oz
Banana Syrup. Fill with
Soda Water.

 **BOYSENBERRY
NUT LATTE**
Pour ½ oz each Syrup:
Boysenberry, Almond.
Add Espresso. Fill with
Foamed/Steamed Milk.

 **BRANDIED
CHERRY LATTE**
Pour ¾ oz Cherry
Syrup, ¼ oz Amaretto
Syrup. Add Espresso.
Fill with Foamed/
Steamed Milk. Splash
with Amaretto Syrup.

# B

 **BRAVE BULL**
Over Ice, Pour 1 oz each Syrup: Coffee, Creme de Cacao. Fill with Soda Water. Splash with Lime Syrup.

 **BRAZIL COOLER**
Over Ice, Pour 1½ oz Apple Syrup, ½ oz Lime Syrup. Fill with Soda Water. Splash with Grenadine Syrup.

 **BREAKFAST EGG NOG COOLER**
Over Ice, Pour 1¼ oz Apricot Syrup. Add Espresso. Fill with Egg Nog. Sprinkle with Nutmeg or Cinnamon.

 **BREVÉ**
Prepare as for latte. Substitute Half-and-Half for Milk.

 **BREVÉ VANILLA**
Pour ¾ oz Vanilla Syrup. Add Espresso. Fill with Foamed/Steamed Half-and-Half.

 **BROWN COW**
Over Ice, Pour ⅔ oz each Syrup: Coffee, Creme de Cacao, Vanilla. Fill with Milk.

 **BROWN VELVET**
Pour ½ oz Creme de Cacao Syrup, ¼ oz Orange Syrup. Add Espresso. Fill with Foamed/Steamed Milk.

 **BULLFROG**
Over Ice, Pour 1 oz Lemon Syrup. Add Espresso. Fill with Milk.

 **BULL'S MILK**
Over Ice, Pour 1½ oz Creme de Cacao Syrup, ½ oz Lime Syrup. Fill with Milk. Sprinkle with Cinnamon or Nutmeg.

# C

###  BUTTER PECAN BREVÉ

Pour ½ oz Thick Butterscotch Syrup, ¼ oz each Syrup: Hazelnut, Almond. Add Espresso. Stir. Fill with Foamed/Steamed Half-and-Half.

### C. C. CRUSH

 Over Ice, Pour 1½ oz Orange Syrup. Fill with Soda Water. Splash with Coconut and Pineapple Syrup.

### CABANA CREAM

 Pour ¾ oz each Syrup: Orange, Banana. Add 1 oz Honey. Stir. Add Ice. Fill with Cold Milk.

### CACAO BANANA CREAM SODA

Over Ice, Pour 1 oz each Syrup: Creme de Cacao, Banana. Add 3 oz Soda Water. Fill with Half-and-Half.

### CADIZ

Over Ice, Pour ¼ oz Apple Syrup, ¾ oz Blackberry Syrup, ½ oz Orange Syrup. Fill with Soda Water to ½" from top of cup. Top with Half-and-Half.

###  CAFE AU LAIT

French version of the latte. 1 or 2 shots of Espresso. Two times as much Foamed Milk.

### CAFE AU CHOCOLATE

Pour ¾ oz Chocolate Syrup. Fill with Hot Water to ½" from top of cup. Top with Espresso and Whipped Cream. Dust with Chocolate Powder.

###  CAFE BON BON

Pour ½ oz Chocolate Mint Syrup, ¼ oz Cherry Syrup. Add Espresso. Top with Foamed/Steamed Milk.

# C

### CAFE CALYPSO
Pour ½ oz Coffee Syrup, ¼ oz Rum Syrup. Fill with Hot Water to ½" from top of cup. Top with Espresso and Whipped Cream.

### CAFE CON LECHE
Spanish version of the latte. 1 or 2 shots of Espresso. 3 times as much Foamed Milk.

### CAFE CONQUISTADOR
Pour ¾ oz Coffee Syrup. Add Espresso. Fill with Foamed/ Steamed Milk. Top with Whipped Cream and Shaved Chocolate.

### CAFÉ CUBANO: MIAMI/ CUBAN VERSION OF ESPRESSO
Pour Espresso in a short cup.

### CAFE DE OLLA
Pour ½ oz Cinnamon Syrup. Add a double shot Espresso. Add 3 oz Hot Water. Top with Steamed Evaporated Milk.

### CAFE DEN DA
Pour a double shot of Espresso. Add Ice. Fill with Cold Water.

### CAFE DI AMARETTO
Pour ¾ oz Amaretto Syrup. Add Espresso. Fill with Foamed/ Steamed Milk. Top with Whipped Cream. Splash with Amaretto Syrup.

### CAFE DIABLO
Pour ½ oz Orange Syrup, ¼ oz Licorice Syrup. Add Hot Water to ½" from top of cup. Top with Espresso. Dust with Mexican Chocolate Powder.

# C

### CAFE FOSTER
Pour ½ oz Rum Syrup, ¼ oz Banana Syrup. Fill with Hot Water to ½" from top of cup. Top with Espresso and Whipped Cream. Splash with Banana Syrup.

### CAFE IBERICO
Pour ½ oz Anisette Syrup, ¼ oz Lemon Syrup. Add Hot Water to 1" from top of cup. Top with a double shot of Espresso.

### CAFE MILCH
German version of the Cappuccino. Simultaneously pour Espresso and Foamed Milk into cup.

### CAFE MUCK
Pour ½ oz Thick Chocolate Syrup, ¼ oz Cherry Syrup. Add a double shot of Espresso. Stir. Top with Whipped Cream. Dust with Chocolate Powder.

### CAFE PUCCI
Pour ½ oz each Syrup: Amaretto, Rum. Fill with Hot Water to ½" from top of cup. Top with Espresso and Whipped Cream.

### CAFE ROMA
Pour a double shot of Espresso. Fill with Foamed/Steamed Milk.

### CAFE SUA DA
Pour a double shot of Espresso. Add Ice. Fill with Sweetened Condensed Milk.

### CAFE THEATRE
Pour ½ oz each Syrup: Creme de Cacao, Irish Cream. Fill with Hot Water to ½" from top of cup. Top with Espresso and Whipped Cream.

### CAFE YUCATAN
Pour ½ oz Creme de Cacao Syrup. Add Espresso. Top with Whipped Cream. Dust with Nutmeg.

# C

 **CAFE VIENNESE**

Pour 2 oz Thick Chocolate Syrup. Add Espresso. Stir. Add 4 oz Cold Water. Add Ice. Fill with Half-and-Half. Dust with Cinnamon and Nutmeg.

 **CAFE ZURICH**

Pour ⅓ oz each Syrup: Amaretto, Anisette, Orange. Fill with Hot Water to ½" from top of cup. Top with Espresso and Whipped Cream.

 **CAFFE NIKKO CREAM SODA**

Over Ice, Pour 1 oz each Syrup: Orange, Creme de Cacao. Fill with Soda Water to ½" from top of cup. Top with Half-and-Half.

 **CAFFE NIKKO ITALIAN SODA**

Over Ice, Pour 1 oz Syrup: Orange, Creme de Cacao. Fill with Soda Water.

 **CAFFE NIKKO STEAMER**

Pour ½ oz each Syrup: Creme de Cacao, Orange. Fill with Foamed/Steamed Milk and top with Whipped Cream. Dust with Chocolate Powder.

 **CAFFE ZINHO**

Add 3 heaping tablespoons Brown Sugar. Fill to ½" from top of cup with Hot Water. Stir. Top with a double shot of Espresso.

 **CALICO JACK**

Over Ice, Pour 1 oz Rum Syrup, ¾ oz Irish Cream Syrup, ¼ oz Lemon Syrup. Fill with Soda Water.

**CALIFORNIA COOLER**

Over Ice, Pour 1 oz each Syrup: Orange, Cherry. Fill with Soda Water.

# C

 **CALIFORNIA SLAMMER**

Over Ice, Pour 1 oz each Syrup: Amaretto, Orange. Fill with Soda Water.

 **CALM VOYAGE**

Over Ice, Pour 1 oz each Syrup: Vanilla, Passion Fruit. Fill with Soda Water to ½" from top of cup. Top with 2 oz Half-and-Half.

 **CALYPSO BREEZE CREAM SODA**

Over Ice, Pour ⅔ oz each Syrup: Kiwi, Passion Fruit, Lemon. Add Soda Water to ½" from top of cup. Top with Half-and-Half.

 **CALYPSO COFFEE**

Pour ¾ oz Rum Syrup. Add Espresso. Fill with Steamed Half-and-Half. Splash with Creme de Cacao Syrup.

 **CALYPSO COOLER**

Pour Espresso. Add Ice. Pour ½ oz each Syrup: Banana, Creme de Cacao, Rum. Fill with Cold Milk. Stir. Dust with Cinnamon Powder.

 **CANADIAN PINEAPPLE**

Over Ice, Pour 1½ oz Pineapple Syrup, ½ oz Lemon Syrup. Fill with Soda Water. Splash with Cherry Syrup.

 **CANADO SALUDO**

Over Ice, Pour ¾ oz each Syrup: Orange, Pineapple. Add ½ oz Lemon Syrup. Fill with Soda Water. Splash with Grenadine Syrup.

 **CANDY APPLE CREAM**

Over Ice, Pour ⅔ oz each Syrup: Apple, Cherry, Cinnamon. Fill with Soda Water to ½" from top of cup. Top with Half-and-Half.

# C

 **CANDY APPLE SODA**

Over Ice, Pour ⅔ oz each Syrup: Apple, Cherry, Cinnamon. Fill with Soda Water.

 **CANDY CANE LATTE**

Pour ¾ oz Cherry Syrup, ¼ oz Mint Syrup. Add Espresso. Fill with Foamed/ Steamed Milk and top with Whipped Cream. Place Candy Cane in the cup to stir.

 **CANEEL BAY CREAM**

Over Ice, Pour 1 oz Rum Syrup. Add ½ oz each Syrup: Coffee, Creme de Cacao. Fill with Soda Water to ¾" from top of cup. Top with Half-and-Half.

 **CANNES-CANNES**

Over Ice, Pour ½ oz Rum Syrup, ⅓ oz Orange Syrup. Add 3 oz Grapefruit Juice. Fill with Soda Water.

 **CAPE CODDER SODA**

Over Ice, Pour 2 oz Cranberry Syrup. Fill with Soda Water. Splash with Lime Syrup.

 **CAPPUCCINO**

First foam and steam Milk. Set pitcher aside. Pour Espresso. Allow Steamed Milk to pour under foam to ½" from top of cup. Top with 2" "cap" of Dense Foam. Dust with Chocolate Powder or Nutmeg.

 **CAPPUCCINO MOCHA**

Pour 1 oz Thick Chocolate Syrup. Foam and steam Milk. Set pitcher aside. Pour Espresso. Stir. Allow Steamed Milk to Pour under Foam to ½" from top of cup. Top with 2" "cap" of Dense Foam. Dust with Chocolate Powder.

# C

 **CAPPUCCINO ALMOND**
Pour ⅓ oz Almond Syrup. Foam and steam Milk. Set pitcher aside. Pour Espresso. Stir. Allow Steamed Milk to pour under Foam to ½" from top of cup. Top with 2" "cap" of Dense Foam. Dust with Chocolate or Vanilla Powder.

 **CAPRI**
Over Ice, Pour 1 oz each Syrup: Creme de Cacao, Banana. Fill with Milk. Sprinkle with Chocolate Powder.

 **CARAMEL ALMOND LATTE**
Pour ½ oz each Syrup: Caramel, Almond. Add Espresso. Fill with Foamed/Steamed Milk.

 **CARAMEL CANDY APPLE CREAM SUPREME**
Over Ice, Pour ½ oz each Syrup: Apple, Boysenberry, Caramel, Cinnamon. Add 3 oz Soda Water. Fill with Half-and-Half. Stir.

 **CARAMEL CREAM SODA**
Over Ice, Pour 1½ oz Caramel Syrup, ½ oz Vanilla Syrup. Fill with Soda Water.

**CARAMEL CREAM STEAMER**
Pour 1 oz Caramel Syrup, ½ oz Vanilla Syrup. Fill with Foamed/Steamed Milk. Top with Whipped Cream.

 **CARAMEL EGG NOG LATTE**
Pour ¾ oz Caramel Syrup. Add Espresso. Fill with Foamed/ Steamed Egg Nog.

# C

## CARAMEL NUT LATTE

Pour ¾ oz Thick Caramel Syrup, ¼ oz Hazelnut Syrup. Add Espresso. Stir. Fill with Foamed/Steamed Milk.

## CARAMEL ROYALE

Pour ⅔ oz Caramel Syrup, ⅓ oz Chocolate Syrup. Add Espresso. Fill with Foamed/ Steamed Milk. Top with Whipped Cream. Garnish with threads of Thick Caramel Syrup over Whipped Cream.

## CARAMELED CINNAMON APPLE LATTE

Pour ½ oz Apple Syrup, ¼ oz each Syrup: Caramel, Cinnamon. Add Espresso. Fill with Foamed/Steamed Milk.

## CARAMELLO

Same as Mocha but substitute Thick Caramel Syrup for Thick Chocolate Syrup.

## CARUMBA

Over Ice, Pour 1 oz each Syrup: Caramel, Rum. Add Soda Water to ½" from top of cup. Fill with Half-and-Half.

## CASA BLANCA COFFEE

Pour ½ oz Amaretto Syrup, ¼ oz Lime Syrup. Add Espresso. Add Foamed/Steamed Milk. Top with Whipped Cream.

## CASINO COOLER

Over Ice, Pour ⅔ oz each Syrup: Lemon, Orange, Cherry. Fill with Soda Water. Top with Whipped Cream.

## CENTER COURT

Over Ice, Pour 1½ oz Strawberry Syrup. Add 2 oz Ginger Ale. Fill to ½" from top of cup with Soda Water. Top with Half-and-Half.

# C

 **CHARIOTS OF FIRE**

Over Ice, Pour 1 oz of
Mandarino Syrup. Fill
to ¾" from top of cup
with Soda Water. Top
with Ginger Ale and
splash with Grenadine
Syrup.

 **CHARLIE CHAPLIN**

Over Ice, Pour 1 oz
each Syrup: Cherry,
Apricot. Fill with Soda
Water. Splash with
Lemon Syrup.

 **CHARTREUSE
SUPREME CREAM
SODA**

Over Ice, Pour 1½ oz
Lime Syrup. Add Soda
Water to ½" from top
of cup. Add ½ oz
Pineapple Syrup. Top
with Half-and-Half and
Whipped Cream.

 **CHERRY
ALEXANDER**

Over Ice, Pour 1 oz
each Syrup: Creme de
Cacao, Cherry. Fill
with Half-and-Half.
Stir.

 **CHERRY BLOSSOM**

Over Ice, Pour 1½ oz
Cherry Syrup. Add
¼ oz each Syrup:
Orange, Lemon. Fill
with Soda Water.
Splash with Grenadine
Syrup.

 **CHERRY BON BON**

Pour ½ oz each Syrup:
Chocolate, Cherry. Add
Espresso. Fill with
Foamed Milk and top
with Chocolate
Sprinkles.

 **CHERRY BRANDY
LATTE**

Pour ½ oz Cherry
Syrup, ¼ oz Amaretto
Syrup. Add Espresso.
Fill with Foamed/
Steamed Milk.

 **CHERRY COBBLER**

Over Ice, Pour 1½ oz
Cherry Syrup, ½ oz
Cinnamon Syrup. Fill
with Soda Water.

 **CHERRY COKE**

Over Ice, Pour ¾ oz
Cherry Syrup. Fill with
Coke.

# C

 **CHERRY COOLER**
Over Ice, Pour 2 oz
Cherry Syrup. Fill with
Soda Water.

 **CHERRY CORDIAL**
Pour ½ oz Cherry
Syrup, ¼ oz each
Syrup: Vanilla,
Almond. Add Espresso.
Fill with Foamed/
Steamed Milk.

 **CHERRY CREAM
TART**
Over Ice, Pour 1½ oz
Cherry Syrup, ½ oz
Lime Syrup. Fill with
Soda Water to ½" from
top of cup. Top with
Half-and-Half.

 **CHERRY DAIQUIRI**
Over Ice, Pour 1 oz
Rum Syrup, ½ oz each
Syrup: Cherry, Lime.
Fill with Soda Water.
Splash with Lime
Syrup.

 **CHERRY FIZZ**
Over Ice, Pour 2 oz
Cherry Syrup. Fill with
Soda Water. Splash
with Lemon Syrup.

 **CHERRY JUBILEE
LATTE**
Pour ½ oz Cherry
Syrup, ¼ oz Vanilla
Syrup. Add Espresso.
Fill with Foamed/
Steamed Milk.

 **CHERRY-LIME
RICKEY**
Over Ice, fill ¾ full
with Soda Water. Add
1 oz each Syrup:
Cherry, Lime. Stir
gently. Float with ¼ oz
Grenadine Syrup.

 **CHERRY COCONUT
LATTE**
Pour ½ oz each Syrup:
Cherry, Coconut. Add
Espresso. Fill with
Foamed/Steamed Milk.

**CHERRY NUT
CREAM SODA**
Over Ice, Pour 1½ oz
Cherry Syrup, ½ oz
Almond Syrup. Fill
with Soda Water to ½"
from top of cup. Top
with Half-and-Half.

# C

###  CHERRY NUT LATTE

Pour ½ oz each Syrup: Cherry, Almond. Add Espresso. Fill with Foamed/Steamed Milk.

###  CHERRY RUM CREAM SODA

Over Ice, Pour 1 oz each Syrup: Cherry, Rum. Fill with Soda Water to ½" from top of cup. Top with Half-and-Half and Whipped Cream.

###  CHI CHI

Over Ice, pour ⅔ oz each Syrup: Rum, Pineapple. Add ½ oz Blackberry Syrup. Fill with Soda Water.

###  CHICAGO COOLER

Over Ice, Pour ½ oz each Syrup: Grape, Lemon. Add Soda Water to ½" from top of cup. Fill with Ginger Ale.

###  CHOCOLATE ALMOND SODA

Over Ice, Pour 1 oz each Syrup: Chocolate, Almond. Fill with Soda Water.

###  CHOCOLATE ANGEL WINGS

Over Ice, Pour 2 oz Chocolate Syrup, 3 oz Soda Water. Fill with Half-and-Half. Top with Whipped Cream.

###  CHOCOLATE CHERRY KISS

Over Ice, Pour 1⅓ oz Cherry Syrup, ⅔ oz Chocolate Syrup, 3 oz Soda Water. Fill with Half-and-Half. Top with Whipped Cream. Dust with Chocolate Powder.

###  CHOCOLATE CHERRY MOCHA

Pour ¾ oz Thick Chocolate Syrup, ⅓ oz Cherry Syrup. Add Espresso. Stir. Fill with Foamed/Steamed Milk. Top with Whipped Cream. Splash with Cherry Syrup.

# C

 **CHOCOLATE EGG CREAM**

Pour 1½ oz Thick Chocolate Syrup, 4 oz Cold Milk. Stir. Add Ice. Fill with Soda Water to ½" from top of cup. Top with ½ oz Vanilla Syrup. Stir again.

 **CHOCOLATE ESPRESSO**

Pour ⅓ oz Chocolate Syrup. Add a double shot Espresso. Stir. Top with dollop of Whipped Cream.

 **CHOCOLATE KAHLUA LATTE**

Pour ½ oz Thick Chocolate Syrup, ½ oz Creme de Cacao Syrup. Add Espresso. Stir. Fill with Foamed/Steamed Milk.

 **CHOCOLATE JAMAICAN**

Over Ice, Pour 1 oz Chocolate Syrup, ½ oz each Syrup: Rum, Amaretto; ¼ oz Almond Syrup. Fill to ½" from top with Milk. Top with Half-and-Half. Dust with Chocolate Powder.

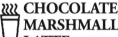 **CHOCOLATE MARSHMALLOW LATTE**

Pour ½ oz each Thick Syrup: Chocolate, Marshmallow. Add Espresso. Stir. Fill with Foamed/Steamed Milk and top with Whipped Cream.

 **CHOCOLATE MINT LATTE**

Pour ¾ oz Chocolate Mint Syrup. Add Espresso. Fill with Foamed/Steamed Milk.

# C

 **CHOCOLATE RUM LATTE**

Pour ½ oz each Syrup: Creme de Cacao, Rum. Add Espresso. Fill with Foamed/Steamed Milk.

**CHOCOLATE MINT CREAM SODA**

Over Ice, Pour 2 oz Chocolate Mint Syrup. Add Soda Water to ½" from top of cup. Fill with Half-and-Half.

 **CHOCOLATE MINT ITALIAN SODA**

Over Ice, Pour 2 oz Chocolate Mint Syrup. Fill with Soda Water.

 **CHOCOLATE RUM SODA**

Over Ice, Pour 1 oz each Syrup: Chocolate, Rum. Fill with Soda Water.

 **CHOCOLATE SHOOTER**

Pour ½ oz Chocolate Syrup in a 4 oz cup. Add Espresso. Stir. Fill with steamed Half-and-Half.

 **CHOCOLATE SPECTACULAR**

Over Ice, Pour 1 oz Chocolate Syrup, ½ oz each Syrup: Coffee, Peach. Add Soda Water to ½" from top of cup. Fill with Half-and-Half. Top with Whipped Cream. Dust with Chocolate Powder.

 **CHOCOLATINO**

Add 1 tablespoon Mexican Chocolate Powder. Add Espresso. Stir. Fill with Foamed/Steamed Milk and Whipped Cream. Dust with Mexican Chocolate Powder.

**CHOCOLATTE**

Pour 1 tablespoon Mexican Chocolate Powder. Add Espresso. Stir. Fill with Foamed/Steamed Milk. Dust with Mexican Chocolate Powder.

# C

 **CHOCONUT EGG NOG LATTE**

Pour ¾ oz Thick Chocolate Syrup. Add Espresso. Stir. Fill with Foamed/Steamed Egg Nog. Dust with Chocolate Powder or Nutmeg.

 **CHRISTMAS CRIMSON COOLER**

Over Ice, Pour 1½ oz Cranberry Syrup, ½ oz Creme de Cassis Syrup. Fill with Soda Water. Splash with Lime Syrup.

 **CINNAMON PEACH LATTE**

Pour ½ oz each Syrup: Cinnamon, Peach. Add Espresso. Fill with Foamed/Steamed Milk.

 **CINNAMON ROLL LATTE**

Pour ½ oz Cinnamon Syrup. Add 1 teaspoon of Brown Sugar. Stir. Add Espresso. Fill with Foamed/Steamed Milk. Top with Whipped Cream. Dust with Cinnamon Powder.

 **CITRUS COOLER**

Over Ice, Pour 1 oz Orange Syrup, ½ oz each Syrup: Lemon, Lime. Fill with Soda Water.

 **CITRUS GROVE SPRITZER**

Over Ice, Pour 1 oz each Syrup: Orange, Lime. Fill with Soda Water. Splash with Grenadine Syrup.

 **CIUDAD COOLER**

Pour Espresso. Add Ice. Fill with Cold Milk or Half-and-Half. Dust with Mexican Chocolate Powder. Add a Cinnamon Stick.

 **CLOVER CLUB CREAM SODA**

Over Ice, Pour 1½ oz Irish Cream Syrup, ½ oz Cinnamon Syrup. Fill to ½" from top of cup with Soda Water. Top with Half-and-Half and ¼ oz Mint Syrup.

# C

 **COCO CHOCO**
Over Ice, Pour 1 oz each Syrup: Coconut, Chocolate. Add Milk to ½" from top of cup. Fill with Half-and-Half.

 **COCO CUSTARD MOCHA**
Pour ½ oz Thick Chocolate Syrup, ¼ oz Vanilla Syrup, splash of Pineapple Syrup. Add Espresso. Stir. Fill with Foamed/Steamed Milk to ¼" from top of cup. Top with Whipped Cream and thin threads of Thick Chocolate Syrup.

 **COCO-MINT ITALIAN SODA**
Over Ice, Pour 2 oz Chocolate Mint Syrup. Fill with Soda Water.

 **COCO-MINT CREAM SODA**
Over Ice, Pour 2 oz Chocolate Mint Syrup. Fill with Soda Water to ½" from top of cup. Top with Half-and-Half.

 **COCO-MOCHO ITALIAN SODA**
Over Ice, Pour 1 oz each Syrup: Coconut, Chocolate. Fill with Soda Water.

 **COCO-MOCHO STEAMER**
Pour ½ oz each Syrup: Coconut, Creme de Cocoa. Fill with Foamed/Steamed Milk. Top with Whipped Cream. Dust with Chocolate Powder.

 **COCO-MOCO**
Pour 1 oz Thick Chocolate Syrup, ⅓ oz Coconut Syrup. Add Espresso. Stir. Fill with Foamed/Steamed Milk. Top with Whipped Cream and Chocolate Sprinkles.

 **COCOA HAZELNUT CREAM COOLER**
Over Ice, Pour 1½ oz Creme de Cacao Syrup, ½ oz Hazelnut Syrup. Fill with Milk.

# C

 **COCOA-COLADA**

Over Ice, Pour ½ oz each Syrup: Creme de Cacao, Rum, Coconut, Pineapple. Add Cold Milk to ½" from top of cup. Top with Half-and-Half.

 **COCONUT AND MANGO LATTE**

Pour ½ oz each Syrup: Coconut, Mango. Add Espresso. Fill with Foamed/Steamed Milk.

 **COCONUT BANANA CREAM**

Over Ice, Pour 1 oz each Syrup: Banana, Coconut. Add Milk to ½" from top of cup. Fill with Half-and-Half.

 **COCONUT BANG**

Over Ice, Pour 1 oz Coconut Syrup. Add ½ oz each Syrup: Orange, Pineapple. Fill with Cold Milk. Splash with Lime Syrup.

 **COCONUT CREAM LATTE**

Pour ½ oz each Syrup: Coconut, Vanilla. Add Espresso. Fill with Foamed/Steamed Milk.

 **COCONUT COFFEE LATTE**

Pour ½ oz each Syrup: Coconut, Coffee. Add Espresso. Fill with Foamed/Steamed Milk.

 **COCONUT COFFEE SMOOTHIE**

Pour Espresso. Add Ice. Add 1 oz Coconut Syrup, ¾ oz Irish Cream Syrup, ¼ oz Coffee Syrup. Fill with Cold Milk.

 **COCONUT CUTIE**

Over Ice, Pour 1⅓ oz Coconut Syrup, ⅔ oz Orange Syrup. Add Soda Water to ½" from top of cup. Fill with Half-and-Half.

# C

 **COCONUT GRAPE LATTE**

Pour ½ oz each Syrup: Coconut, Grape. Add Espresso. Fill with Foamed/Steamed Milk.

 **COCONUT KISS**

Over Ice, Pour 1¼ oz Coconut Syrup, ¾ oz Pineapple Syrup. Add Soda Water to ½" from top of cup. Fill with Half-and-Half. Splash with Grenadine Syrup.

 **COCONUT LIPS**

Over Ice, Pour 1 oz Coconut Syrup, ½ oz each Syrup: Pineapple, Raspberry. Add Soda Water to ½" from top of cup. Fill with Half-and-Half. Splash with Raspberry Syrup.

 **COCONUT MOCHA**

Pour ½ oz Coconut Syrup, 1½ oz Thick Chocolate Syrup. Add Espresso. Stir. Fill with Foamed/Steamed Milk. Top with Whipped Cream and Chocolate Powder.

 **COFFEE ALEXANDER**

Pour Espresso. Add Ice. Add 1¼ oz Creme de Cacao. Top with 2 oz Half-and-Half.

 **COFFEE COOLER**

Pour Espresso. Add Ice. Add 1 oz Irish Cream Syrup. Fill with Cold Water to ½" from top of cup. Top with Half-and-Half.

 **COFFEE EGG NOG**

Pour Espresso. Add Ice. Add 4 oz Cold Water. Fill with Egg Nog. Stir.

 **COFFEE GRASSHOPPER**

Over Ice, Pour 1½ oz Creme de Menthe Syrup. Add Espresso. Fill with Milk. Stir.

**COFFEE NOGGIN**

Pour ¾ oz Creme de Cacao Syrup. Add Espresso. Fill with Steamed Half-and-Half. Sprinkle with Powdered Nutmeg.

# C

## COFFEE NUDGE

Pour ½ oz each Syrup: Creme de Cacao, Coffee. Add ⅛ oz Mandarino Syrup. Fill to ¾" from top with Hot Water. Add Espresso. Top with Whipped Cream. Dust with Nutmeg.

## COFFEE NUT

Pour ½ oz Hazelnut Syrup, ¼ oz Orange Syrup. Add 6 oz Hot Water. Add Espresso. Top with Whipped Cream.

## COFFEE SCOTCH

Pour 2 oz Thick Butterscotch Syrup. Add Espresso. Stir. Fill with Hot Water.

## COFFEE SOUR

Over Ice, Pour 1½ oz Lemon Syrup. Add Espresso. Fill with Soda Water.

## COLADA BRAZIL

Over Ice, Pour ⅔ oz each Syrup: Chocolate, Pineapple; ⅓ oz each Syrup: Passion Fruit, Rum. Add Soda Water to ½" from top of cup. Fill with Half-and-Half.

## COLUMBIA CLUB SODA

Over Ice, Pour 1 oz each Syrup: Raspberry, Rum. Fill with Soda Water. Splash with Lemon Syrup.

## COOLER

Over Ice, Pour 2 oz any Flavored Syrup. Fill with Soda Water.

## COPACABANA CREAM SODA

Over Ice, Pour ⅔ oz each Syrup: Chocolate, Passion Fruit, Rum. Add Soda Water to ½" from top of cup. Fill with Half-and-Half.

# C

 **COSSACK COFFEE GROG**

Pour Espresso. Add Ice. Pour ¾ oz Creme de Cacao Syrup. Add ½ oz each Syrup: Chocolate, Vanilla. Fill with Cold Milk. Dust with Cinnamon Powder.

 **COUNTRY CLUB COOLER**

Over Ice, Pour 1½ oz Apple Syrup, ½ oz Grenadine Syrup. Fill with Soda Water.

 **COZUMEL COFFEE COOLER**

Pour double shot of Espresso. Add Ice. Add 1 oz Orange Syrup, ½ oz Rum Syrup. Fill with Cold Water.

 **CRANBERRY COOLER**

Over Ice, Pour 2 oz Cranberry Syrup. Fill with Soda Water. Splash with Orange Syrup.

 **CRANBERRY CREAM SODA**

Over Ice, Pour 1½ oz Cranberry Syrup, ½ oz Vanilla Syrup. Add Soda Water to ½" from top of cup. Fill with Half-and-Half.

 **CRANBERRY GRAPE COOLER**

Over Ice, Pour 1 oz each Syrup: Cranberry, Grape. Fill with Soda Water.

 **CRANBERRY JUBILEE SODA**

Over Ice, Pour 1 oz Cranberry Syrup, ½ oz each Syrup: Lemon, Coconut. Fill with Soda Water.

 **CRANBERRY SCENTED SPARKLING CIDER**

Over Ice, Pour 6 oz Apple Juice, ½ oz Cranberry Syrup. Splash with Lime Syrup.

# C

 **CRANBERRY SPARKLER**

Over Ice, Pour 2 oz Cranberry Syrup. Fill with Soda Water. Splash with Lemon Syrup.

 **CRANBERRY TANGERINE CREAM SODA**

Over Ice, Pour 1 oz each Syrup: Cranberry, Mandarino. Add Soda Water to ½" from top of cup. Fill with Half-and-Half.

 **CREAM PUFF SODA**

Over Ice, Pour 1 oz each Syrup: Vanilla, Coconut. Fill with Milk to ½" from top of cup. Top with Whipped Cream. Dust with Vanilla Powder.

 **CREAM SODA**

Over Ice, Pour 2 oz Vanilla Syrup. Fill with Soda Water.

 **CREAMCICLE**

Over Ice, Pour 1 oz each Syrup: Orange, Vanilla. Fill with Half-and-Half to ½" from top of cup. Top with Soda Water. Stir.

 **CREAMY MALIBU COFFEE**

Pour ½ oz Pineapple Syrup, ¼ oz each Syrup: Rum, Coconut. Add Espresso. Fill with Steamed Milk.

 **CREME DE CAFE**

Over Ice, Pour 1 oz Coffee Syrup. Add ½ oz each Syrup: Amaretto, Anisette. Fill with Milk. Top with Whipped Cream.

**CREME DE MENTHE COOLER**

Over Ice, Pour 2 oz Creme de Menthe Syrup. Fill with Soda Water.

# C

 **CREOLE LEMONADE**

Over Ice, Pour 1½ oz Lemon Syrup, ½ oz Pineapple Syrup. Fill with Soda Water. Splash with Strawberry Syrup.

 **CRIMSON SLIPPER**

Over Ice, Pour 1½ oz Cherry Syrup, ½ oz Lemon Syrup. Fill with Soda Water.

 **CRYSTAL SPRINGS ORANGE SODA**

Over Ice, Pour 1 oz each Syrup: Orange, Apple. Fill with Soda Water. Splash with Grenadine Syrup.

 **CUBA LIBRE**

Over Ice, Pour 1 oz Rum Syrup, ⅓ oz Lime Syrup. Fill with Cola.

 **CUBAN HOT COFFEE**

Pour ½ oz Rum Syrup, ¼ oz Creme de Cacao Syrup. Add Hot Water to 1" from top of cup. Top with a double shot of Espresso.

 **DAIQUIRI COOLER**

Over Ice, Pour ⅓ oz Rum Syrup, ⅔ oz Lime Syrup. Fill with Soda Water. Splash with Lime Syrup.

 **DATE NUT DREAM CREAM**

Over Ice, Pour 1 oz each Syrup: Tamarindo, Hazelnut. Add Soda Water to ½" from top of cup. Fill with Half-and-Half.

 **DEMPSEY COOLER**

Over Ice, Pour 1½ oz Apple Syrup, ½ oz Anisette Syrup. Fill with Soda Water. Splash with Grenadine Syrup.

 **DENISE**

Pour a triple shot of Espresso. Add Ice. Add 1 oz Vanilla Syrup. Fill with 1% Milk.

 **DOPPIO**

Double shot of Espresso with 1 measure (shot) of Water.

# D

## DOUBLE

Double measure of Espresso with double measure of Water.

## DOUBLE DECADENCE

Pour ½ oz Thick Chocolate Syrup, ¾ oz Caramel Syrup. Add Espresso. Stir. Fill with Foamed/Steamed Chocolate Milk. Top with Whipped Cream, and Thin Threads of Thick Chocolate Syrup.

## DOUBLE NO FUN

A latte made with a double shot of Decaf Espresso and Nonfat Milk.

## DOUBLE SHORT HARMLESS FOAMLESS

In an 8 oz cup, Pour double shot Decaf Espresso. Fill with Steamed Milk, no Foam.

## DOUBLE STANDARD

A latte made with Decaf Espresso and Foamed/Steamed Half-and-Half.

## DOUBLE TALL SKINNY BILLIARD BALL

Same as a "Double Tall Skinny Foamless."

## DOUBLE TALL SKINNY FOAMLESS

A tall latte made with a double shot of Espresso and Nonfat Steamed Milk. No Foam.

## DOUBLE TALL SKINNY LATTE

A tall latte made with a double shot of Espresso and Nonfat Milk.

## DOUBLE TALL SPLIT

Pour 1 Shot of Regular Espresso and 1 Shot of Decaf Espresso. Fill with Foamed/ Steamed Milk.

# D

## DOUBLE TALL TWO

A tall latte made with a double shot of Espresso and 2% Milk.

## DOUBLE TALL WHIPLESS

A tall mocha with a double shot of Espresso and no Whipped Cream.

## DOUBLE TALL

A tall latte with a double shot of Espresso.

## DOUG'S DOWNUNDER

Over Ice, Pour ⅔ oz each Syrup: Kiwi, Passion Fruit, Coconut. Fill with Soda Water.

## DREAM CREAM— CREAM SODA

Over Ice, Pour 1⅓ oz Orange Syrup, ⅔ oz Vanilla Syrup. Add 3 oz Soda Water. Fill with Half-and-Half.

## DREAM CREAM ITALIAN SODA

Over Ice, Pour 1⅓ oz Orange Syrup, ⅔ oz Vanilla Syrup. Fill with Soda Water.

## DREAM CREAM STEAMER

Pour ½ oz each Syrup: Orange, Vanilla. Fill with Foamed/Steamed Milk. Top with Whipped Cream. Dust with Vanilla Powder.

## DROP KICK

Pour 5 oz Hot Water. Top with double shot of Espresso.

## DRY CAPPUCCINO

First foam and steam Milk. Set pitcher aside. Pour Espresso. Reach into pitcher with spatula and pull out dense Foam to fill and top with 2" "cap" of Foam. Dust with Chocolate Powder or Nutmeg.

# E

## DUTCH CHOCOLATE ALMOND LATTE

Pour ½ oz each Syrup:
Chocolate Mint,
Almond. Add Espresso.
Fill with Foamed/
Steamed Milk.

## DUTCH COFFEE

Pour ¾ oz Chocolate
Mint Syrup. Add 5 oz
Hot Water and
Espresso. Top with
Whipped Cream.

## EAST INDIA COOLER

Over Ice, Pour ⅔ oz
each Syrup: Coffee,
Orange, Pineapple. Fill
with Soda Water.

## EASTER EGG HATCH

Over Ice, Pour ⅓ oz
each Syrup: Irish
Cream, Vanilla,
Orange. Fill with Egg
Nog. Sprinkle with
Nutmeg.

## EGG NOG CAPPUCCINO

Fill steam pitcher ⅓
full with equal parts of
Egg Nog and Milk.
Foam and steam Egg
Nog-Milk mixture. Set
pitcher aside. Pour
Espresso. Allow
steamed Egg Nog-Milk
mixture to pour under
foam to ½" from top of
cup. Top with 2" "cap"
of dense Foam. Dust
with Chocolate Powder
or Nutmeg.

## EGG NOG LATTE

Pour Espresso. Fill with
Foamed/Steamed Egg
Nog. Dust with
Cinnamon or Nutmeg
Powder.

## EGG NOG MOCHA

Pour 1½ oz Thick
Chocolate Syrup. Add
Espresso. Stir. Fill with
Foamed/Steamed Egg
Nog. Dust with
Nutmeg.

# E

 **EGG NOG STEAMER**
Fill with Foamed/ Steamed Egg Nog. Top with Whipped Cream. Sprinkle with Nutmeg.

 **EL PRESIDENTE COOLER**
Over Ice, Pour ⅔ oz each Syrup: Lime, Pineapple, Cherry. Fill with Soda Water.

 **EMERALD ZOMBIE**
Over Ice, Pour ½ oz each Syrup: Melon, Mint, Coconut, Pineapple. Fill with Soda Water.

 **ESPRESSO**
Pour Espresso in a short cup.

 **ESPRESSO CHERRY FLIP**
Pour ¾ oz Cherry Syrup. Add 8 oz Hot Water. Top with Espresso and Whipped Cream.

 **ESPRESSO CON GHIACCIO**
In an 8 oz cup, Pour Espresso. Fill to ½" from top with Ice. Add 1½ oz of Cold Milk.

 **ESPRESSO CON GHIACCIO E LATTE**
Pour Ice into short cup and add 2 oz Cold Milk. In separate short cup, Pour Espresso.

 **ESPRESSO CON PANNA**
Pour Espresso in a short cup. Top with a dollop of Whipped Cream.

 **ESPRESSO EGG NOG**
Pour Espresso. Add Ice. Fill with Egg Nog. Stir. Dust with Powdered Nutmeg.

# E

## ESPRESSO GRAND ROYAL

Pour ½ oz each Syrup: Orange, Lemon. Add Espresso. Add lots of Steamed Milk and a short layer of Foamed Milk. Top with Whipped Cream. Splash with Cherry Syrup.

## ESPRESSO MANDARINO

Pour ½ oz Mandarino Syrup. Add Espresso.

## ESPRESSO NUDGE

Pour ½ oz Creme de Cacao Syrup, ¼ oz Mandarino Syrup, 2 oz Hot Water. Add a double shot Espresso. Dust with Cinnamon and Nutmeg. Add Cinnamon Stick.

## ESPRESSO ROMANO

Pour Espresso. Add a Twist of Lemon in a short cup.

## ESPRESSO SPICED APPLE

Pour ½ oz Apple Syrup, ¼ oz Cinnamon Syrup. Add 8 oz Hot Water. Top with Espresso.

## ESPRESSO TROPICANA

Pour a double shot of Espresso. Add Ice. Add 1½ oz Rum Syrup, ½ oz Coconut Syrup. Add 2 oz Half-and-Half. Top with Soda Water.

## EYE-OPENER

Pour ¾ oz Anisette Syrup. Add a double shot Espresso. Fill with Foamed/Steamed Milk.

## FANTASIA

Pour 1 oz of any Flavored Syrup. Fill with Foamed Milk. Dust with Nutmeg.

## FERRARI

Over Ice, Pour 1½ oz Cherry Syrup, ½ oz Amaretto Syrup. Fill with Soda Water.

# F

 **FIFTH AVENUE COOLER**

Over Ice, Pour 1 oz each Syrup: Apricot, Creme de Cacao. Fill with Soda Water to ½" from top of cup. Top with Half-and-Half.

 **FLAMINGO CANARY**

Over Ice, Pour 1⅓ oz Strawberry Syrup, ⅔ oz Lemon Syrup. Fill with Soda Water.

 **FLAMINGO FLAME SODA**

Over Ice, Pour ½ oz Apple Syrup. Add Grapefruit Juice to ½" from top of cup. Top with ⅓ oz Cherry Syrup.

 **FLAVORED CAPPUCCINO**

Pour 1 oz Flavored Syrup into a steaming pitcher. Add 6-8 oz Cold Milk. Foam and steam the Milk-Syrup mixture. Set pitcher aside. Pour Espresso. Allow flavored Steamed Milk to pour under Foam to ½" from top of cup. Top with 2" "cap" of Foam. Dust with any Flavored Powder.

 **FLORADORA COOLER**

Over Ice, Pour 1 oz each Syrup: Lime, Orange. Fill with Soda Water. Splash with Grenadine Syrup.

 **FLYING GRASSHOPPER**

Over Ice, Pour 1⅓ oz Creme de Menthe Syrup, ½ oz Creme de Cacao Syrup. Fill with Soda Water.

# F

 **FLYING KANGAROO**

Over Ice, Pour ½ oz each Syrup: Coconut, Pineapple, Orange; ¼ oz each Syrup: Banana, Rum. Add Soda Water to ½" from top of cup. Fill with Half-and-Half.

 **FOG CUTTER**

Over Ice, Pour ⅔ oz each Syrup: Creme de Cacao, Orange, Almond. Fill with Soda Water.

 **FRAPPE**

Over Ice, Pour 2 oz any Flavored Syrup. Fill glass halfway with Soda Water.

 **FRENCH COLADA**

Over Ice, Pour ⅔ oz each Syrup: Coconut, Pineapple; ⅓ oz each Syrup: Creme de Cassis, Rum. Add Soda Water to ½" from top of cup. Fill with Half-and-Half.

**FRENCH VANILLA LATTE**

Pour ½ oz Vanilla Syrup, ¼ oz Hazelnut Syrup. Add Espresso. Fill with Foamed/Steamed Milk and top with Whipped Cream. Dust with Vanilla Powder.

 **FRITZER**

Over Ice, Pour 1 oz Lemon Syrup. Fill with Soda Water or Ginger Ale. Splash with Grenadine Syrup.

 **FROSTED MINT LATTE**

Pour ¾ oz Mint Syrup. Add Espresso. Fill with Foamed/Steamed Milk.

 **FRUIT FANTASIA**

Over Ice, Pour ⅔ oz each Syrup: Watermelon, Pineapple, Coconut. Add Soda Water to ½" from top of cup. Fill with Half-and-Half. Splash with Grenadine Syrup.

# G

## FUZZY LEMON FIZZ

Over Ice, Pour 1½ oz Lemon Syrup, ½ oz Peach Syrup. Fill with Soda Water. Splash with Grenadine Syrup.

## FUZZY NAVEL

Over Ice, Pour 1¼ oz Peach Syrup, ¾ oz Orange Syrup. Fill with Soda Water. Splash with Grenadine Syrup.

## GENTLE SEA BREEZE

Over Ice, Pour 1 oz Cranberry Syrup. Fill with Grapefruit Juice. Splash with Cranberry Syrup.

## GEORGIA DREAM CREAM SODA

Over Ice, Pour 1¼ oz Peach Syrup, ½ oz Vanilla Syrup, ¼ oz Lemon Syrup. Add Soda Water to ½" from top of cup. Fill with Half-and-Half. Splash with Lime Syrup.

## GEORGIA MINT JULEP

Over Ice, Pour 1¾ oz Peach Syrup, ¼ oz Mint Syrup. Fill with Milk. Top with Whipped Cream. Splash with Mint Syrup.

## GEORGIA RUM COOLER

Over Ice, Pour 1¼ oz Rum Syrup, ½ oz Grenadine Syrup, ¼ oz Lemon Syrup. Fill with Soda Water. Splash with Praline Syrup.

## GERMAN CHOCOLATE MOCHA

Pour ½ oz Thick Chocolate Syrup, ¼ oz Thick Caramel Syrup. Add ¼ oz each Syrup: Coconut, Hazelnut. Add Espresso. Stir. Fill with Foamed/Steamed Milk. Top with Whipped Cream and Chocolate Sprinkles.

# G

 **GINGER MINT COOLER**

Over Ice, Pour 1 oz Mint Syrup. Add 4 oz Ginger Ale. Fill with Soda Water.

 **GINGER ORANGE CREAM**

Over Ice, Pour 1 oz Orange Syrup. Add Ginger Ale to ½" from top of cup. Fill with Half-and-Half.

 **GLACIER SODA**

Over Ice, Pour 1¼ oz Anisette Syrup, ¾ oz Peppermint Syrup. Fill with Soda Water.

 **GLOOM LIFTER**

Pour Espresso. Add Ice. Pour 1 oz Raspberry Syrup, ½ oz Lemon Syrup. Fill with Milk.

 **GOING APE**

Pour ¾ oz Thick Chocolate Syrup. Add ⅓ oz Banana Syrup. Add Espresso. Stir. Fill with Foamed/Steamed Milk and top with Whipped Cream and Chocolate Sprinkles.

 **GOLDEN DAWN**

Over Ice, Pour 1 oz Apple Syrup. Add ½ oz each Syrup: Apricot, Orange. Fill with Soda Water. Splash with Grenadine Syrup.

 **GOLDEN FLAMINGO FIZZ**

Over Ice, Pour 1½ oz Cherry Syrup. Fill to ¼" from top of cup with Soda Water. Top with ½ oz Lemon Syrup.

 **GOLDEN SLIPPER**

Over Ice, Pour ⅔ oz Lemon Syrup, 1⅓ oz Apricot Syrup. Fill with Soda Water.

 **GOLDEN SOMBRERO FIZZ**

Pour 1½ oz Apple Syrup, ½ oz Cinnamon Syrup, ½ oz Honey. Stir. Add Ice. Fill with Soda Water. Splash with Lemon Syrup.

# G

 **GRAND ROYAL FIZZ**

Over Ice, Pour ½ oz each Syrup: Coffee, Lemon, Maraschino, Orange. Add Half-and-Half to ½" from top of cup. Fill with Soda Water.

 **GRANITA**

A machine-made slush drink flavored with sugar and either a coffee or fruit essence. A milk or nondairy cream base can be added.

 **GRANOLA BAR LATTE**

Pour ⅓ oz each Thick Syrup: Honey, Molasses. Add ½ oz Coconut Syrup. Add Espresso. Stir. Fill with Foamed/Steamed Milk and Whipped Cream.

 **GRAPE & LIME COOLER**

Over Ice, Pour 1 oz each Syrup: Grape, Lime. Fill with Soda Water.

 **GRAPE BERRY CREAM SODA**

Over Ice, Pour 1 oz each Syrup: Grape, Blueberry. Add Soda Water to ½" from top of cup. Fill with Half-and-Half.

 **GRAPE CREAM SODA**

Over Ice, Pour 1 oz each Syrup: Grape, Vanilla. Add Soda Water to ½" from top. Fill with Half-and-Half.

 **GRAPE CRUSH**

Over Ice, Pour 1⅓ oz Grape Syrup. Add ⅓ oz each Syrup: Cranberry, Lime. Fill with Soda Water.

 **GRAPE NUT LATTE**

Pour ½ oz each Syrup: Grape, Almond. Add Espresso. Fill with Foamed/Steamed Milk.

# H

 **GRASSHOPPER CREAM COOLER**

Over Ice, Pour 1⅓ oz Creme de Menthe Syrup, ⅔ oz Creme de Cacao Syrup. Add 3 oz Soda Water. Fill with Half-and-Half.

 **GREEN DEVIL COOLER**

Over Ice, Pour 1½ oz Creme de Menthe Syrup, ½ oz Lime Syrup. Fill with Soda Water.

 **GREEN DRAGON COOLER**

Over Ice, Pour 1½ oz Creme de Menthe Syrup, ½ oz Lemon Syrup. Fill with Soda Water.

 **GREEN OPAL**

Over Ice, Pour 1½ oz Lime Syrup, ½ oz Anisette Syrup. Fill with Soda Water.

 **HAMMERHEAD**

Pour a double shot of Espresso. Add 5 oz French-roast Coffee.

 **HARLEM COOLER**

Over Ice, Pour 1½ oz Pineapple Syrup, ½ oz Maraschino Syrup. Fill with Soda Water.

 **HARVARD COOLER**

Over Ice, Pour 2 oz Apple Syrup. Fill with Soda Water.

 **HAVANA CREAM COOLER**

Over Ice, Pour ⅔ oz each Syrup: Coffee, Pineapple, Lime. Fill with Soda Water to ½" from top of cup. Top with 2 oz Half-and-Half.

 **HAVANA SPECIAL**

Over Ice, Pour 1¼ oz Pineapple Syrup, ¾ oz Rum Syrup. Fill with Soda Water. Splash with ¼ oz Grenadine Syrup.

# H

###  HAWAIIAN DELIGHT

Over Ice, Pour 1 oz each Syrup: Pineapple, Coconut. Fill with Soda Water to ½" from top of cup. Top with Half-and-Half.

###  HAWAIIAN ESPRESSO

Pour Espresso. Into a steaming pitcher, Pour 1 oz Coconut Syrup and 6 oz Cold Milk. Foam and steam the Flavored Milk. Top the Espresso with equal parts of Steamed and Foamed Flavored Milk.

###  HAWAIIAN ICED COFFEE

Pour Espresso. Add Ice. Add ⅔ oz each Syrup: Pineapple, Passion Fruit, Coconut. Fill with Milk. Top with Whipped Cream.

### HAZELNUT DIVINITY LATTE

Pour ½ oz Hazelnut Syrup, ¼ oz Creme de Cacao Syrup. Stir in 1 teaspoon Dutch Chocolate Powder. Pour Espresso. Stir. Fill with Foamed/Steamed Milk.

### HAZELNUT HOT CHOCOLATE

Pour 1¼ oz Thick Chocolate Syrup, ¼ oz Hazelnut Syrup. Fill with Foamed/Steamed Milk. Stir. Top with Whipped Cream. Dust with Chocolate Powder.

### HAZELNUT LATTE

Pour ¾ oz Hazelnut Syrup. Add Espresso. Fill with Foamed/ Steamed Milk.

### HAZELNUT TRUFFLE LATTE

Pour ½ oz Thick Chocolate Syrup, ½ oz Hazelnut Syrup. Add Espresso. Stir. Fill with Foamed/Steamed Milk.

# H

 **HIGHBALL SODA**
Over Ice, Pour 1 oz
each Syrup: Lemon,
Mint. Fill with Soda
Water.

 **HONEY ESPRESSO**
Pour 1¼ oz Honey.
Add 8 oz Hot Water
and stir. Top with
Espresso.

 **HONEY ICED
ESPRESSO**
In 8 oz cup, Pour
Espresso. Add Ice. Add
2 oz of Half-and-Half.
Add tablespoon of
Honey. Stir.

 **HONEY VANILLA
CREAM LATTE**
Pour ¾ oz Honey, ⅓ oz
Vanilla Syrup. Add
Espresso. Stir. Fill with
Foamed/Steamed Milk.

 **HONOLULU
COOLER**
Over Ice, Pour ⅔ oz
each Syrup: Orange,
Pineapple, Passion
Fruit. Fill with Soda
Water.

**HOT AFTER
DINNER MINT
STEAMER**
Pour ½ oz each Syrup:
Creme de Menthe,
Chocolate. Fill with
Foamed/Steamed Milk.
Top with Whipped
Cream.

**HOT APPLE PIE**
Pour ¾ oz Apple
Syrup. Add ¼ oz each
Syrup: Hazelnut,
Cinnamon. Add 6 oz
Hot Water. Add
Espresso.

**HOT BRICK
TODDY**
Pour ¾ oz Praline
Syrup. Add Espresso.
Fill with Foamed/
Steamed Milk.

**HOT BUTTERED
RUM LATTE**
Pour ½ oz Rum Syrup,
¼ oz Thick
Butterscotch Syrup.
Add Espresso. Stir. Fill
with Foamed/Steamed
Milk.

# H

### HOT BUTTERED COFFEE
Place 1 tablespoon Brown Sugar, 1 tablespoon Soft Butter in cup. Add pinch of Cinnamon, and a pinch of Nutmeg Powder. Add Hot Water to 1" from top of cup. Stir. Top with Espresso.

### HOT CHOCOLATE
Pour 2 oz Thick Chocolate Syrup. Fill with Foamed/Steamed Milk. Stir. Top with Whipped Cream and dust with Chocolate Powder.

### HOT CHOCOLATE BANANA
Pour ½ oz each Syrup: Chocolate, Banana. Fill with Foamed/Steamed Milk and top with Whipped Cream and Powdered Chocolate.

### HOT COCONUT COFFEE
Pour ¾ oz Coconut Syrup. Add Hot Water to ½" from top of cup. Top with Espresso.

### HOT GOLD
Pour ½ oz each Syrup: Amaretto, Orange. Add Espresso. Fill with Foamed/Steamed Milk.

### HOT MOCHA HONEY
Pour ¾ oz Thick Chocolate Syrup. Add ¾ oz Honey. Add Espresso. Stir. Fill with Foamed/Steamed Milk. Top with Whipped Cream and Chocolate Powder.

### HOT SPICED CRANBERRY
In an 8 oz cup, Pour ½ oz each Syrup: Cranberry, Rum. Add ¼ oz Cinnamon Syrup. Fill with Hot Water. Dust with Nutmeg.

### HOT SPRINGS COOLER
Over Ice, Pour 2 oz Pineapple Syrup. Fill with Soda Water. Splash with Maraschino Syrup.

# I

 **HOT TODDY**
Steam 8 oz Apple Juice. Pour into cup. Add ½ teaspoon Brown Sugar. Stir. Dust with Cinnamon.

 **HUMMER**
Over Ice, Pour ⅔ oz each Syrup: Chocolate, Coffee, Rum. Add Soda Water to ½" from top of cup. Fill with Half-and-Half.

 **HURRICANE SODA**
Over Ice, Pour 1 oz each Syrup: Apple, Pineapple. Fill with Soda Water. Splash with Grenadine Syrup.

 **ICED BREVÉ**
Pour Espresso. Add Ice. Fill with Half-and-Half.

**ICED CAPPUCCINO**
Pour Espresso. Add Ice. Fill with Milk. Top with Whipped Cream. Dust with Nutmeg.

 **ICED CHOCOLATE ALMOND MOO**
Over Ice, Pour 1 oz each Syrup: Chocolate, Almond. Fill with Cold Milk. Dust with Chocolate Powder.

 **ICED CHOCOLATE ESPRESSO**
Pour 1½ oz Chocolate Syrup. Add Espresso. Fill with Ice. Add Cold Milk to ½" from top of cup. Top with Whipped Cream. Place one Chocolate-covered Coffee Bean on top.

 **ICED COFFEE**
Over Ice, Pour Espresso. Fill with Cold Water.

 **ICED COFFEE ROYALE**
Over Ice, Pour 1 oz Coffee Syrup, ½ oz Chocolate Syrup, ¼ oz each Syrup: Coconut, Vanilla. Fill to ¼" from top of cup with Soda Water. Top with Half-and-Half.

# I

###  ICED BREVÉ LATTE

Pour Espresso. Fill with Ice. Top with Half-and-Half.

###  ICED BREVÉ MOCHA

Pour 2 oz Thick Chocolate Syrup. Add Espresso. Stir. Fill with Ice. Pour Half-and-Half to ½" from top of cup. Top with Whipped Cream and Chocolate Sprinkles.

###  ICED ESPRESSO

Use a short cup. Pour Espresso. Add Ice.

###  ICED LATTE

Pour Espresso. Add Ice. Fill with Milk.

###  ICED MOCHA

Pour 2 oz Thick Chocolate Syrup. Add Espresso. Stir. Add Ice. Fill with Milk. Top with Whipped Cream and Chocolate Sprinkles.

###  ICED RUM COFFEE

Pour 1½ oz Rum Syrup. Add Espresso. Fill with Ice. Fill with Milk. Splash with Coffee Syrup.

###  ICY MINTY MOCHA

Pour 1½ oz Thick Chocolate Syrup, 1 oz Mint Syrup. Add Espresso. Stir. Add Ice. Fill with Milk. Top with Whipped Cream and Chocolate Sprinkles.

###  IMPERIAL EGG NOG

Over Ice, Pour 1 oz Amaretto Syrup. Fill with Cold Egg Nog. Stir. Dust with Powdered Nutmeg.

###  INDIAN SUMMER

Over Ice, Pour 2 oz Apple Syrup. Fill with Soda Water. Add Cinnamon Stick.

# I

 **INDIAN SUMMER 2**
Over Ice, Pour 1 oz
Vanilla Syrup. Add
Apple Cider to ½"
from top of cup. Fill
with Soda Water. Add
Cinnamon Stick.

 **INNOCENT
PASSION**
Over Ice, Pour 1 oz
Passion Fruit Syrup,
½ oz each Syrup:
Cranberry, Lemon. Fill
with Soda Water.

 **IRISH COFFEE**
Pour ¾ oz Irish Cream
Syrup. Add Espresso.
Fill with Hot Water.
Top with Whipped
Cream.

 **IRISH COW
STEAMER**
Pour 1 oz Irish Cream
Syrup. Fill with
Foamed/Steamed Milk.
Top with Whipped
Cream.

**IRISH CREAM
BREVÉ**
Pour ¾ oz Irish Cream
Syrup. Add Espresso.
Fill with Foamed/
Steamed Half-and-
Half.

**IRISH CREAM EGG
NOG LATTE**
Pour ¾ oz Irish Cream
Syrup. Add Espresso.
Fill with Foamed/
Steamed Egg Nog.
Dust with Chocolate
Powder.

**IRISH ESPRESSO**
Pour ¾ oz Irish Cream
Syrup. Add 8 oz Hot
Water. Top with
Espresso.

**IRISH NUT**
Pour ½ oz each Syrup:
Hazelnut, Irish Cream.
Add Espresso. Fill with
Steamed Milk. Dust
with Nutmeg.

# I

###  I.R.S. CREAM SODA

Over Ice, Pour ⅔ oz each Syrup: Cherry, Lime, Pineapple. Add Soda Water to ½" from top of cup. Fill with Half-and-Half. Top with Whipped Cream. Garnish with Money Umbrella.

###  ISLAND COOLER

Over Ice, Pour ½ oz each Syrup: Orange, Mango, Passion Fruit, Pineapple. Fill with Soda Water. Splash with Cranberry Syrup.

###  ITALIAN COLADA

Over Ice, Pour ⅔ oz each Syrup: Coconut, Pineapple, ⅓ oz each Syrup: Amaretto, Rum. Add Soda Water to ½" from top of cup. Fill with Half-and-Half.

###  ITALIAN COFFEE

Pour ¾ oz Amaretto Syrup. Add Hot Water to 1" from top of cup. Top with double shot of Espresso.

###  ITALIAN CREAM SODA

Over Ice, Pour 2 oz of any Flavored Syrup. Add Soda Water to ½" from top of cup. Fill with Half-and-Half.

###  ITALIAN SODA

Over Ice, Pour 2 oz of any Flavored Syrup. Fill with Soda Water.

###  ITALIAN SOMBRERO

Pour ¾ oz Amaretto Syrup. Add Espresso. Fill with Foamed/ Steamed Half-and-Half.

###  JAMAICA FEVER

Over Ice, Pour ½ oz each Syrup: Pineapple, Mango, Cherry, Rum. Fill with Soda Water. Splash with Lime Syrup.

###  JAMAICA HOP

Pour ½ oz each Syrup: Coffee, Creme de Cacao. Add a double shot Espresso. Fill with Foamed/Steamed Milk.

# J

## JAMAICAN BANANA CREAM LATTE

Pour ½ oz Banana Syrup, ¼ oz each Syrup: Rum, Coconut. Add Espresso. Fill with Foamed/Steamed Milk. Splash with Creme de Cacao Syrup.

## JAMAICAN COFFEE

Pour ½ oz Coffee Syrup, ¼ oz Praline Syrup, 5 oz Hot Water. Add Espresso. Top with Whipped Cream. Dust with Nutmeg.

## JAMAICAN LATTE

Pour ½ oz each Syrup: Cinnamon, Creme de Cacao. Add Espresso. Fill with Foamed/Steamed Milk.

## JAPANESE LATTE

Pour ⅓ oz each Syrup: Cherry, Orange, Almond. Add Espresso. Fill with Foamed/Steamed Milk.

## JELLY BEAN LATTE

Pour ½ oz each Syrup: Anisette, any Fruit Flavor. Add Espresso. Fill with Foamed/Steamed Milk.

## JELLY BEAN SODA

Over Ice, Pour 1 oz each Syrup: Anisette, any Fruit Flavor. Fill with Soda Water.

## KAFFEE MILCH

A German latte, made with Viennese roast. The espresso and steamed milk are generally poured into a large ceramic mug simultaneously.

## KAHLUA EGG CREAM

Over Ice, Pour 2 oz Coffee Syrup. Add Cold Milk to 1" from top of cup. Fill with Soda Water.

# K

### KAHLUA ALMOND FUDGE LATTE

Pour ½ oz each Syrup: Almond, Chocolate. Add Espresso. Fill with Foamed/Steamed Milk. Dust with Chocolate Powder.

### KAHLUA ALMOND FUDGE SODA

Over Ice, Pour ⅔ oz each Syrup: Coffee, Almond, Chocolate. Fill with Soda Water.

### KAHLUA COFFEE

Pour ¾ oz Creme de Cacao Syrup. Add 5 oz Hot Water. Add Espresso. Top with Whipped Cream. Dust with Nutmeg.

### KAHLUA & CREAM

Pour ¾ oz Creme de Cacao Syrup. Add Espresso. Fill with Foamed/Steamed Half-and-Half.

### KAHLUA & CREAM COOLER

Pour Espresso. Add Ice. Pour 1½ oz Creme de Cacao Syrup. Fill with Half-and-Half.

### KAHLUA EGG NOG LATTE

Pour ¾ oz Creme de Cacao Syrup. Add Espresso. Fill with Foamed/Steamed Egg Nog. Dust with Chocolate Powder or Nutmeg.

### KAHLUA LATTE

Pour ¾ oz Coffee Syrup. Add Espresso. Fill with Foamed/Steamed Milk.

### KAHLUA-N-CREAM BREVÉ

Pour ¾ oz Coffee Syrup. Add Espresso. Fill with Foamed/Steamed Half-and-Half. Top with Whipped Cream and splash with Coffee Syrup.

# L

 **KEY LIME CREAM SODA**

Over Ice, Pour 1½ oz Lime Syrup, ½ oz Vanilla Syrup. Add Soda Water to ½" from top of cup. Top with Half-and-Half and Whipped Cream.

 **KIWI & CREAM SODA**

Over Ice, Pour 1 oz each Syrup: Kiwi, Vanilla. Add Soda Water to ½" from top of cup. Fill with Half-and-Half.

 **KIWI & GINGER SPRITZER**

Over Ice, Pour 1 oz Kiwi Syrup. Fill with equal parts Ginger Ale and Soda Water.

 **KLONDIKE COOLER**

Over Ice, Pour ⅓ oz each Syrup: Orange, Apricot, Pineapple. Fill with Ginger Ale.

**LACCINO**

A latte-cappuccino combination, with less milk and more foam than a standard latte.

**LAKE BREEZE**

Over Ice, Pour ⅔ oz each Syrup: Strawberry, Cranberry. Add ⅓ oz each syrup: Lemon, Pineapple. Fill with Soda Water.

**LATTE**

Pour Espresso. Fill with Foamed/Steamed Milk.

**LATTE CALDO**

Fill cup with Hot Steamed Milk.

**LATTE MACCHIATO**

Pour Steamed Milk to ½" from top of cup. Top with Peak of Foamed Milk. Pour Espresso through Milk leaving a telltale marking.

# L

## LATTE ROYALE
Pour ¾ oz any Flavored Syrup. Add Espresso. Fill with Steamed Milk to ¼" from top of cup. Top with Flavored Whipped Cream and any garnish.

## LATTECCINO
Pour Espresso. Fill with ⅔ Steamed Milk and ⅓ Foamed Milk.

## LEMON AND LIME SODA
Over Ice, Pour 1 oz each Syrup: Lemon, Lime. Fill with Soda Water.

## LEMON CHIFFON CREAM PIE SODA
Over Ice, Pour 1⅓ oz Lemon Syrup, ⅔ oz Vanilla Syrup. Fill with Soda Water to ½" from top of cup. Top with Half-and-Half and Whipped Cream.

## LEMON CHILL
Over Ice, Pour 2 oz Lemon Syrup. Fill with Soda Water.

## LEMON ESPRESSO
Pour ¼ oz Lemon Syrup in cup. Add a double shot of Espresso.

## LEMON RUM COFFEE
Pour ⅓ oz each Syrup: Lemon, Rum. Add Hot Water to 1" from top of cup. Top with Espresso.

## LEPRECHAUN
Pour ½ oz Irish Cream Syrup, ¼ oz Mint Syrup. Add Espresso. Fill with Foamed/ Steamed Milk. Top with Whipped Cream.

## LIME & MINT JULEP
Over Ice, Pour 1 oz each Syrup: Lime, Mint. Fill with Soda Water.

## LIME COLA COOLER
Over Ice, Pour ½ oz Lime Syrup. Fill with Cola.

# M

 **LIME COOLER**
Over Ice, Pour 2 oz
Lime Syrup. Fill with
Soda Water.

 **LIME RICKEY**
Over Ice, Pour 2 oz
Lime Syrup. Fill with
Soda Water. Splash
with Cherry Syrup.

 **LUNGO (Long Pour)**
Pour 1½ oz Water
through a Single
Measure of Espresso—
7 grams.

 **MACCHIATO**
Pour Espresso. Top
with a dollop of
Foamed Milk in a small
cup.

 **MADRAS COOLER**
Over Ice, Pour 1 oz
each Syrup: Orange,
Cranberry. Fill with
Soda Water.

 **MAI TAI COOLER**
Over Ice, Pour 1 oz
Rum Syrup. Add ¼ oz
each Syrup: Almond,
Orange, Lime. Fill with
Soda Water to ½" from
top of cup. Top with
¼ oz Grenadine Syrup.

 **MAIDEN'S BLUSH
SODA**
Over Ice, Pour 1 oz
each Syrup: Mango,
Lemon. Fill with Soda
Water. Splash with
Grenadine Syrup.

 **THE MAIN ISLAND
SODA**
Over Ice, Pour 1 oz
each Syrup: Banana,
Pineapple. Fill with
Soda Water. Splash
with Strawberry Syrup.

*Chapter 2—Recipes*    89

# M

 **MALTED MOCHA**

Pour 1 heaping teaspoon of Malt Powder into a cup. Add 1 oz Thick Chocolate Syrup. Add Espresso. Stir. Fill with Foamed/ Steamed Milk. Top with Whipped Cream and Chocolate Sprinkles.

 **MANGO COOLER**

Over Ice, Pour 2 oz Mango Syrup. Fill with Soda Water.

**MANDARINO LIME SODA**

Over Ice, Pour 1⅓ oz Mandarino Syrup, ⅔ oz Lime Syrup. Fill with Soda Water.

 **MANGO & COCONUT CREAM SODA**

Over Ice, Pour 1 oz each Syrup: Mango, Coconut. Add Soda Water to ½" from top of cup. Fill with Half-and-Half. Splash with Grenadine Syrup.

 **MANGO MELBA**

Over Ice, Pour ⅔ oz each Syrup: Mango, Banana, Raspberry. Add Soda Water to ½" from top of cup. Fill with Half-and-Half.

 **MANGO NUT LATTE**

Pour ½ oz each Syrup: Mango, Hazelnut. Add Espresso. Fill with Foamed/Steamed Milk.

 **MANGO ORANGE CREAM SODA**

Over Ice, Pour 1 oz each Syrup: Mango, Orange. Fill with Soda Water to ½" from top of cup. Top with Half-and-Half. Splash with Mango Syrup.

 **MANILA FIZZ**

Over Ice, Pour ¾ oz Lime Syrup. Add Egg Nog to 1" from top of cup. Fill with Root Beer.

# M

## MAPLE LATTE

Pour ¾ oz Maple Syrup. Add Espresso. Fill with Foamed/Steamed Milk.

## MAPLE MOCHA

Pour ½ oz Maple Syrup, ¾ oz Thick Chocolate Syrup. Add Espresso. Stir. Fill with Foamed/Steamed Milk. Top with Whipped Cream and Chocolate Sprinkles.

## MARADONA CREAM COOLER

Over Ice, Pour 1¾ oz Passion Fruit Syrup, ¼ oz Coconut Syrup. Add Soda Water to ½" from top of cup. Fill with Half-and-Half.

## MARVIN'S CAPPUCCINO NEAPOLITAN

Pour ½ oz each Syrup into steaming pitcher: Strawberry, Vanilla. Add Milk to pitcher until ⅓ full. Foam and steam Milk-Syrup. Set pitcher aside. Pour ⅓ oz Chocolate Syrup into cup. Add Espresso to cup. Stir. Allow steamed Milk-Syrup to pour under foam to ½" from top of cup. Top with 2" "cap" of Dense Foam. Dust with Chocolate Powder.

## MARZIPAN ORANGE BREVÉ

Pour ¾ oz Orange Syrup, ¼ oz Amaretto Syrup. Add Espresso. Top with Foamed/Steamed Half-and-Half.

# M

 **MAUI COOLER**

Over Ice, Pour ⅔ oz Pineapple Syrup, ½ oz Vanilla Syrup. Add Soda Water to ½" from top of cup. Fill with Orange Juice. Splash with Grenadine Syrup.

 **MAY BLOSSOM FIZZ**

Over Ice, Pour ⅔ oz each Syrup: Cherry, Almond, Strawberry. Fill with Soda Water. Splash with Lemon Syrup.

 **MAZAGRAN AMERICANO**

Pour ¾ oz Lemon Syrup. Add Espresso. Add Ice. Fill with Soda Water.

 **MacINTOSH APPLE SODA**

Over Ice, Pour 1 oz each Syrup: Apple, Lemon. Fill with Soda Water. Splash with Cherry Syrup.

 **MEDITERRANEAN COFFEE**

Pour ¼ oz each Syrup: Chocolate, Anisette. Add 4 oz Hot Water. Add Espresso. Top with Whipped Cream.

 **MEGA MOCHA**

A standard mocha with a double shot espresso in a 16 oz cup.

 **MELLOW YELLOW CREAM SODA**

Over Ice, Pour 1 oz each Syrup: Lemon, Vanilla. Add Soda Water to ½" from top of cup. Fill with Half-and-Half. Splash with Banana Syrup.

 **MELON BALL**

Over Ice, Pour 1 oz each Syrup: Melon, Pineapple. Fill with Soda Water.

 **MELONADE**

Over Ice, Pour 1 oz Melon Syrup. Add ½ oz each Syrup: Orange, Lime. Fill with Soda Water.

# M

 **MERRY WIDOW FIZZ**

Over Ice, Pour ⅓ oz each Syrup: Lemon, Orange. Add ⅔ oz Cherry Syrup. Add Egg Nog to 1" from top of cup. Fill with Soda Water. Splash with Grenadine Syrup.

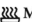 **MEXICAN COFFEE**

Pour double shot of Espresso. Fill with Steamed Milk. Dust with Cinnamon.

 **MEXICAN COFFEE 2**

Pour ¾ oz Coffee Syrup. Fill to ½" from top with Hot Water. Top with Espresso and Whipped Cream. Dust with Mexican Chocolate Powder.

 **MEXICAN COLADA**

Over Ice, Pour ⅔ oz each Syrup: Coconut, Pineapple; ⅓ oz each Syrup: Creme de Cacao, Rum. Add Soda Water to ½" from top of cup. Fill with Half-and-Half.

**MEXICAN HOT CHOCOLATE**

Same as hot chocolate except with Mexican chocolate mix (a blend of chocolate, cinnamon, nutmeg, and almonds).

**MEXICAN MELANGE LATTE**

Pour ¼ oz each Syrup: Amaretto, Coconut, Banana, Cinnamon. Add Espresso. Fill with Foamed/Steamed Milk.

**MEXICAN MOCHA**

Pour 1 oz Thick Chocolate Syrup. Add 1 tablespoon Mexican Chocolate Powder. Add Espresso. Stir. Fill with Foamed/Steamed Milk. Top with Whipped Cream and Mexican Chocolate Powder.

# M

### MEXICAN MUDSLINGER

Pour ½ oz Creme de Cacao Syrup, ¼ oz Coffee Syrup. Add Espresso. Fill with Foamed/Steamed Half-and-Half. Splash with Coffee Syrup.

### MEXICOLA

Over Ice, Pour ½ oz Lime Syrup. Fill with Cola. Splash with Lime Syrup.

### MIDNIGHT SILK MOCHA

Pour ½ oz each Syrup: Anisette, Chocolate. Add Espresso. Add Foamed/Steamed Milk. Top with Whipped Cream.

### MILE HIGH BANANA CREAM CAPPUCCINO

Pour ½ oz Banana Syrup into serving cup. Pour ¾ oz Banana Syrup into steaming pitcher. Add 6 oz Cold Milk. Foam and steam Milk-Syrup mixture. Set pitcher aside. Pour Espresso. Allow Flavored Steamed Milk to pour under foam to ½" from top of cup. Top with 2" "cap" of Dense Foam.

### MILE HIGH ORANGE BANANA CREAM

Over Ice, Pour 1 oz each Syrup: Orange, Banana. Add Soda Water to ½" from top of cup. Fill with Half-and-Half. Top with lots of Whipped Cream. Splash with Grenadine Syrup.

# M

**MILKY WAY ICED**
Over Ice, Pour 1 oz
each Syrup: Caramel,
Chocolate. Fill with
Soda Water to ½" from
top of cup. Top with
Half-and-Half and
Whipped Cream.

**MILKY WAY**
Pour ¾ oz of each
Thick Syrup: Caramel,
Chocolate. Add
Espresso. Stir. Fill with
Foamed/Steamed Milk.
Top with Whipped
Cream and Chocolate
Sprinkles.

**MIMOSA**
Over Ice, Pour 1 oz
each Syrup: Orange,
Apple. Fill with Soda
Water.

**MINT COOLER**
Over Ice, Pour 2 oz
Creme de Menthe
Syrup. Fill with Soda
Water.

**MINT CREAM
COLADA**
Over Ice, Pour ¾ oz
each Syrup: Coconut,
Pineapple. Add Soda
Water to ½" from top
of cup. Fill with Half-
and-Half. Splash with
¼ oz Mint Syrup.

**MINT CREAM
SODA**
Over Ice, Pour 2 oz
Creme de Menthe
Syrup, 3 oz Soda Water.
Fill with 2 oz Half-and-
Half. Top with
Whipped Cream.

**MINT DREAM
TEAM**
Over Ice, Pour 2 oz
Creme de Menthe
Syrup. Fill to ½" from
top with Soda Water.
Top with Half-and-
Half and Whipped
Cream.

# M

 **MINT JULEP**

Over Ice, Pour 2 oz
Mint Syrup. Fill with
Milk. Top with
Whipped Cream.
Splash with Mint
Syrup.

 **MINT PATTY**

Pour ½ oz each Syrup:
Creme de Cacao,
Creme de Menthe. Fill
with Hot Water to ½"
from top of cup. Add
Espresso. Top with
Whipped Cream.

**MINTY LEMON
ESPRESSO**

Pour ⅓ oz each Syrup:
Lemon, Mint. Add Hot
Water to 1" from top of
cup. Top with Espresso.

 **MIXED FRUIT
SMOOTHY**

Over Ice, Pour 1 oz
each Syrup: Orange,
Peach. Add Soda Water
to ½" from top of cup.
Fill with Half-and-
Half. Splash with
Vanilla Syrup.

 **MOCHA**

Pour 1 oz Thick
Chocolate Syrup. Add
Espresso. Stir. Fill with
Foamed/Steamed Milk.
Top with Whipped
Cream and Chocolate
Sprinkles.

 **MOCHA & CREAM**

Over Ice, Pour 1¼ oz
Coffee Syrup, ¾ oz
Creme de Cacao Syrup.
Fill with Half-and-
Half. Top with
Whipped Cream.

 **MOCHA CREAM
COOLER**

Over Ice, Pour 1 oz
Creme de Cacao Syrup.
Add Espresso and 3 oz
Soda Water. Fill with
Half-and-Half. Top
with Whipped Cream.

**MOCHA FROTH**

Pour 1 oz Thick
Chocolate Syrup. Add
Espresso. Stir. Fill with
Foamed Milk. Dust
with Chocolate Powder.

# M

### 🎵 MOCHA LITE

Pour 1 heaping tablespoon of Sugarfree Cocoa into cup. Add Espresso. Stir. Fill with Foamed/Steamed Nonfat Milk.

### 🎵 MOCHA MINT

Pour ¾ oz Thick Chocolate Syrup, ¼ oz Creme de Menthe Syrup. Add Espresso. Stir. Fill with Foamed/ Steamed Milk. Top with Whipped Cream and Chocolate Sprinkles.

### 🎵 MOCHA MINT LATTE

Pour ¾ oz Thick Chocolate Syrup, ⅓ oz Creme de Menthe Syrup. Add Espresso. Stir. Fill with Foamed/ Steamed Milk. Top with Whipped Cream and Chocolate Sprinkles.

### 🎵 MOCHA MOO

Pour ⅓ oz Almond Syrup, ¾ oz Thick Chocolate Syrup. Add Espresso. Stir. Fill with Foamed/Steamed Milk. Top with Whipped Cream and Chocolate Sprinkles.

### 🎵 MOCHA STEAMER

Pour 1 oz Creme de Cacao Syrup. Fill with Foamed/Steamed Milk. Top with Whipped Cream and dust with Chocolate Powder.

### 🎵 MOCK MOOSE MILK

Pour 1 oz Rum Syrup, ½ oz Almond Syrup. Fill with Foamed/ Steamed Milk.

### 🎵 MOONLIGHT SODA

Over Ice, Pour 1⅓ oz Apple Syrup, ⅔ oz Lemon Syrup. Fill with Soda Water.

# M

**MORNING GLORY FIZZ**

Over Ice, Pour 1¼ oz Lemon Syrup, ¾ oz Anisette Syrup. Fill with Soda Water.

**MOUNDS® BAR**

Over Ice, Pour 1 oz each Syrup: Chocolate, Coconut. Add 2 oz Soda Water. Fill with Half-and-Half. Stir.

**MOUNDS® BAR LATTE**

Pour 1 oz Thick Chocolate Syrup, ⅓ oz Coconut Syrup. Add Espresso. Stir. Fill with Foamed/Steamed Milk. Top with Whipped Cream and thin threads of Thick Chocolate Syrup.

**MT. ST. HELENS**

In an 8-oz cup, Pour a triple shot of Espresso. Top with Whipped Cream.

**MUD SLIDE**

Pour 1½ oz Thick Chocolate Syrup. Add a double shot of Espresso. Stir. Fill with Steamed Milk. Top with Whipped Cream and Chocolate Sprinkles.

**NEW ORLEANS COFFEE**

(Use a very Dark Roast, or Chicory Blend, Coffee.) Pour double shot of Espresso. Fill with Steamed Milk.

**NEWTON SPRITZER**

Over Ice, Pour 2 oz Apple Syrup. Fill with Soda Water. Splash with Lemon Syrup.

**NIENTA**

First foam and steam Nonfat Milk. Set pitcher aside. Pour Decaf Espresso. Allow Steamed Milk to pour under Foam to ½" from top of cup. Top with 2" "cap" of dense Foam. Dust with Chocolate Powder or Nutmeg.

# N

###  NO FUN
A latte with Decaf Espresso.

### NUTTIN' HONEY LATTE
Pour 1 tablespoon Honey, ½ oz Hazelnut Syrup. Add Espresso. Stir. Fill with Foamed/Steamed Milk. Dust with Nutmeg Powder.

### NUTTY BUDDY
Pour ¾ oz Thick Chocolate Syrup and ⅓ oz Hazelnut Syrup. Add Espresso. Stir. Fill with Foamed/Steamed Milk.

### NUTTY CARAMEL COFFEE
Pour ½ oz Caramel Syrup, ¼ oz Hazelnut Syrup. Add 4 oz Hot Water and top with Espresso.

### NUTTY COCADA CREAM SODA
Over Ice, Pour ⅔ oz each Syrup: Amaretto, Coconut, Pineapple. Add Soda Water to ½" from top of cup. Top with Half-and-Half.

### OLD FASHIONED AMERICAN SODA
Over Ice, Pour 1 oz Vanilla Syrup and 1 oz of any other Flavored Syrup. Fill with Soda Water.

### OLD FASHIONED COBBLER CREAM SODA
Over Ice, Pour ⅔ oz each Syrup: Apple, Peach. Add ½ oz Cinnamon Syrup and 3 oz Soda Water. Fill with Half-and-Half. Top with Whipped Cream.

### OLYMPIC GOLD SODA
Over Ice, Pour 1¼ oz Passion Fruit Syrup, ¾ oz Strawberry Syrup. Fill with Soda Water.

# O

### ORANGE ALMOND LATTE

Pour ½ oz each Syrup: Orange, Almond. Add Espresso. Fill with Foamed/Steamed Milk.

### ORANGE ALMOND MOCHA

Pour ¾ oz Thick Chocolate Syrup. Add ¼ oz each Syrup: Orange, Almond. Add Espresso. Stir. Fill with Foamed/Steamed Milk. Top with Whipped Cream and Chocolate Sprinkles.

### ORANGE BANANA CREAM SODA

Over Ice, Pour ¾ oz each Syrup: Orange, Banana. Add ½ oz Vanilla Syrup. Add Soda Water to ½" from top of cup. Fill with Half-and-Half.

### ORANGE BRANDY LATTE

Pour ½ oz Orange Syrup, ¼ oz Amaretto Syrup. Add Espresso. Fill with Foamed/Steamed Milk.

### ORANGE COFFEE

Pour ¾ oz Orange Syrup. Add Hot Water to ½" from top of cup. Top with Espresso.

### ORANGE DROP ITALIAN SODA

Over Ice, Pour ¾ oz each Syrup: Cherry, Lemon, ½ oz Orange Syrup. Fill with Soda Water.

### ORANGE EGG NOG LATTE

Pour ¾ oz Orange Syrup. Add Espresso. Fill with Foamed/Steamed Egg Nog and top with Whipped Cream.

### ORANGE FIZZ

Over Ice, Pour 1½ oz Orange Syrup, ½ oz Lime Syrup. Fill with Soda Water.

# O

 **ORANGE FLOWER COOLER**

Over Ice, Pour 1 oz Orange Syrup. Add 3 oz Grapefruit Juice. Fill with Soda Water. Splash with Maraschino Syrup.

 **ORANGE GROG**

Pour into steam pitcher, 1 oz Orange Syrup, ½ oz Cinnamon Syrup. Add 9 oz Water. Steam. Pour into cup. Dust with Cinnamon Powder.

 **ORANGE IRISH CREAM LATTE**

Pour ½ oz each Syrup: Orange, Irish Cream. Add Espresso. Fill with Foamed/Steamed Milk.

 **ORANGE MOCHA**

Pour ¾ oz Thick Chocolate Syrup, ⅓ oz Orange Syrup. Add Espresso. Stir. Fill with Foamed/Steamed Milk. Top with Whipped Cream and Chocolate Sprinkles.

 **ORANGE NUT LATTE**

Pour ½ oz Orange Syrup, ¼ oz Hazelnut Syrup. Add Espresso. Fill with Foamed/ Steamed Milk.

 **ORANGE OASIS**

Over Ice, Pour 1½ oz Orange Syrup, ½ oz Cherry Syrup. Fill with Soda Water.

 **ORANGE SPARKLER**

Over Ice, Pour 1½ oz Orange Syrup, ½ oz Anisette Syrup. Fill with Soda Water.

 **ORANGE SWIZZLE**

Over Ice, Pour 1½ oz Orange Syrup. Add Soda Water to ½" from top of cup. Fill with Ginger Ale. Splash with Grenadine Syrup.

 **OVALTINE LATTE**

Pour 1 heaping tablespoon of Ovaltine into cup. Add Espresso. Stir. Fill with Foamed/ Steamed Milk.

# O

###  OUTRIGGER
Over Ice, Pour ⅔ oz
each Syrup: Peach,
Lime, Pineapple. Fill
with Soda Water.

###  PAGO PAGO
Over Ice, Pour 1 oz
Rum Syrup, ½ oz
Pineapple Syrup, ¼ oz
each Syrup: Creme de
Cacao, Lime. Fill with
Soda Water. Splash
with Lime Syrup.

###  PALISADES SODA
Over Ice, Pour 1 oz
Banana Syrup. Add
Soda Water to 1 ½"
from top of cup. Fill
with Orange Juice.

###  PALM GROVE COOLER
Over Ice, Pour ½ oz
each Syrup: Orange,
Mango, Pineapple,
Lime. Fill with Soda
Water. Splash with
Grenadine Syrup.

###  PANAMA COOLER
Over Ice, Pour ⅔ oz
each Syrup: Chocolate,
Banana, Coffee. Fill
with Soda Water.

###  PARADISE COOLER
Over Ice, Pour ½ oz
each Syrup: Orange,
Lemon, Banana, Rum.
Fill with Soda Water.

###  PARK AVENUE ICED ESPRESSO
Pour Espresso. Add Ice.
Add 1 oz Vanilla Syrup.
Fill with Soda Water.

###  PASSION FRUIT SPRITZER
Over Ice, Pour 2 oz
Passion Fruit Syrup.
Fill with Soda Water.

###  PASSION NUT LATTE
Pour ½ oz Passion Fruit
Syrup, ¼ oz Hazelnut
Syrup. Add Espresso.
Fill with Foamed/
Steamed Milk.

# P

 **PEACH & GINGER SPRITZER**

Over Ice, Pour 1 oz Peach Syrup. Add Soda Water to ¾" from top of cup. Fill with Ginger Ale.

 **PEACH & LIME COOLER**

Over Ice, Pour 1½ oz Peach Syrup, ½ oz Lime Syrup. Fill with Soda Water.

 **PEACH BLOSSOM**

Over Ice, Pour 1½ oz Peach Syrup, ½ oz Almond Syrup. Fill with Soda Water. Splash with Grenadine Syrup.

 **PEACH BUNNY**

Over Ice, Pour 1 oz each Syrup: Peach, Creme de Cacao. Add Soda Water to ½" from top of cup. Top with Half-and-Half.

 **PEACH COCONUT FLIP**

Over Ice, Pour 1 oz Peach Syrup, ¼ oz Rum Syrup, ¾ oz Coconut Syrup. Add Soda Water to ½" from top of cup. Fill with Half-and-Half.

 **PEACH MELBA**

Over Ice, Pour 1½ oz Peach Syrup, ½ oz Raspberry Syrup. Add Soda Water to ½" from top of cup. Fill with Half-and-Half.

 **PEACH ORANGE & GINGER FIZZ**

Over Ice, Pour ⅔ oz each Syrup: Peach, Orange. Fill with equal parts of Ginger Ale and Soda Water.

 **PEACH SANGAREE**

Over Ice, Pour 1½ oz Peach Syrup, ½ oz Grape Syrup. Fill with Soda Water. Splash with Lemon Syrup.

# P

 **PEACH SCHNAPPS COOLER**

Over Ice, Pour 1½ oz Peach Syrup, ½ oz Amaretto Syrup. Fill with Soda Water.

 **PEACH SCHNAPPS LATTE**

Pour ½ oz Peach Syrup, ¼ oz Amaretto Syrup. Add Espresso. Fill with Foamed/Steamed Milk.

 **PEACH-ANISETTE AND LIME COOLER**

Over Ice, Pour ⅔ oz each Syrup: Peach, Anisette, Lime. Fill with Soda Water.

 **PEACHES-N-CREAM**

Over Ice, Pour 2 oz Peach Syrup. Fill with Soda Water to ½" from top of cup. Top with Half-and-Half and Whipped Cream.

 **PEACHLIFTER**

Over Ice, Pour ¾ oz Peach Syrup. Add ½ oz each Syrup: Apple, Lime, Coconut. Fill with Soda Water.

 **PEANUT BAR MOCHA**

Pour ½ oz Thick Chocolate Syrup. Add 1 tablespoon Smooth Peanut Butter. Add Espresso. Stir. Fill with Foamed/Steamed Milk to ¼" from top of cup. Top with Whipped Cream and Thin Threads of Thick Chocolate Syrup.

 **PEANUT BUTTER CUP**

Pour ½ oz Thick Chocolate Syrup. Add 1 tablespoon Peanut Butter. Add Espresso. Stir. Fill with Foamed/ Steamed Milk. Top with Whipped Cream and Chocolate Sprinkles.

 **PEANUT BUTTER-CARAMEL COFFEE**

Pour ⅔ oz Caramel Syrup. Add 1 tablespoon Peanut Butter. Add Espresso. Stir. Add Ice. Fill with Cold Milk.

# P

 **PEDRO COLLINS**
Over Ice, Pour 1⅓ oz
Rum Syrup, ⅔ oz
Lemon Syrup. Fill with
Soda Water.

 **PEPPERMINT
CREAM TWIST**
Over Ice, Pour 1½ oz
Peppermint Syrup. Add
Soda Water to ½" from
top of cup. Fill with
Half-and-Half to ¼"
from top of cup. Top
with ½ oz Cherry
Syrup.

 **PEPPERMINT
PATTY**
Over Ice, Pour 1 oz
each Syrup:
Peppermint, Creme de
Cacao. Add Soda Water
to ½" from top of cup.
Fill with Half-and-
Half.

 **PEPPERMINT
PATTY SODA**
Over Ice, Pour 1 oz
each Syrup:
Peppermint, Creme de
Cacao. Fill with Soda
Water.

 **PEPPERMINT
VANILLA LATTE**
Pour ½ oz each Syrup:
Peppermint, Vanilla.
Add Espresso. Fill with
Foamed/Steamed Milk.

 **PEPPY PENGUIN**
Pour 1½ oz Thick
Chocolate Syrup. Add a
double shot of Espresso.
Stir. Add Ice. Fill with
Half-and-Half.

 **PERPETUALLY
YOURS**
Over Ice, Pour 1½ oz
Creme de Cassis, ½ oz
Creme de Cacao. Fill
with Soda Water.

 **PINA COLADA
CREAM SODA**
Over Ice, Pour 1 oz
each Syrup: Coconut,
Pineapple. Add 2 oz
Soda Water. Fill with
Half-and-Half.

 **PIÑATA**
Over Ice, Pour 1½ oz
Banana Syrup, ½ oz
Lime Syrup. Add 3 oz
Soda Water. Fill with
Half-and-Half.

# P

 **PINEAPPLE COOLER**

Over Ice, Pour 2 oz Pineapple Syrup. Fill with Soda Water. Splash with Grenadine Syrup.

 **PINEAPPLE CRANBERRY SPRITZER**

Over Ice, Pour 1 oz each Syrup: Pineapple, Cranberry. Fill with equal parts Ginger Ale and Soda Water.

 **PINEAPPLE MINT COOLER**

Over Ice, Pour 1¼ oz Pineapple Syrup, ½ oz Creme de Menthe Syrup, ¼ oz Lemon Syrup. Fill with Soda Water.

 **PINEAPPLE RUM FIZZ**

Over Ice, Pour 1 oz each Syrup: Pineapple, Rum. Fill with Soda Water.

 **PINK ALMOND CREAM SODA**

Over Ice, Pour 1 oz each Syrup: Almond, Cherry. Add Soda Water to ½" from top of cup. Fill with Half-and-Half. Splash with Cherry Syrup.

 **PINK CREOLE SODA**

Over Ice, Pour ⅔ oz each Syrup: Grenadine, Lime, Rum. Fill with Soda Water.

 **PINK ELEPHANT**

Over Ice, Pour 1 oz Grenadine Syrup. Add ½ oz each Syrup: Lemon, Lime. Fill with Soda Water.

 **PINK FLAMINGO**

Over Ice, Pour 1 oz Strawberry Syrup. Add ⅓ oz each Syrup: Apple, Lemon, Banana. Fill with Soda Water.

 **PINK LADY**

Over Ice, Pour 1¾ oz Raspberry Syrup, ¼ oz Lemon Syrup. Fill with Soda Water.

# P

 **PINK PANTHER**

Over Ice, Pour 1 oz
each Syrup: Creme de
Cassis, Mandarino.
Add Soda Water to ½"
from top of cup. Fill
with Half-and-Half.

 **PINK PANTHER SODA**

Over Ice, Pour 1 oz
each Syrup: Cherry,
Pineapple. Fill with
Soda Water. Splash
with Grenadine Syrup.

 **PINK PUSSY CAT**

Over Ice, Fill cup to
½" from top with
Grapefruit Juice. Add
½ oz Grenadine Syrup.

 **PINK SNOWMAN**

Over Ice, Pour ⅔ oz
each Syrup: Raspberry,
Orange, Vanilla. Add
Soda Water to ¾" from
top of cup. Top with
Half-and-Half.

 **PINK SQUIRREL**

Over Ice, Pour 1 oz
Cherry Syrup, ⅔ oz
Almond Syrup, ⅓ oz
Creme de Cacao Syrup.
Add 3 oz Soda Water.
Fill with Half-and-
Half.

 **PINKY COLADA**

Over Ice, Pour ⅔ oz
each Syrup: Coconut,
Pineapple, Grenadine.
Add Soda Water to ½"
from top of cup. Fill
with Half-and-Half.
Splash with Grenadine
Syrup.

 **POCA POLA**

Over Ice, Pour 1 oz
Tamarindo Syrup. Fill
with Ginger Ale. Splash
with Lemon Syrup.

 **POLLYANNA**

Over Ice, Pour ⅔ oz
each Syrup:
Mandarino, Pineapple,
Raspberry. Fill with
Soda Water.

# P

 **POLYNESIAN CREAM SODA**

Over Ice, pour ¾ oz each Syrup: Rum, Passion Fruit. Pour ½ oz Lime Syrup. Add Soda Water to ½" from top of cup. Top with Half-and-Half. Splash with Lime Syrup.

 **POPSICLE**

Over Ice, Pour 1 oz Amaretto Syrup, Add Orange Juice to ½" from top of cup. Fill with Half-and-Half.

 **POSTEM LATTE**

Add 1 heaping teaspoon Postem. Pour 2 oz Hot Water. Stir. Fill with Foamed/Steamed Milk.

 **PRALINE LATTE**

Pour ¾ oz Praline Syrup. Add Espresso. Fill with Foamed/Steamed Milk.

 **PRALINE MOCHA**

Pour ¾ oz Thick Chocolate Syrup, ⅓ oz Praline Syrup. Add Espresso. Stir. Fill with Foamed/Steamed Milk. Top with Whipped Cream and Chocolate Sprinkles.

 **PRALINE SPRITZER**

Over Ice, Pour 2 oz Praline Syrup. Fill with Soda Water. Splash with Orange Syrup.

**PRALINES & CREAM LATTE**

Pour ½ oz Praline Syrup, ¼ oz Vanilla Syrup. Add Espresso. Fill with Foamed/Steamed Milk.

 **PRESBYTERIAN**

Over Ice, Pour 1½ oz Irish Cream Syrup. Fill with equal parts of Ginger Ale and Soda Water.

# P

 **PRETTY MAMA**

Over Ice, Pour 1 oz
each Syrup: Apricot,
Pineapple. Add Soda
Water. Splash with
Grenadine Syrup.

 **PRETTY MAMA
CREAM SODA**

Over Ice, Pour 1 oz
each Syrup: Apricot,
Pineapple. Add Soda
Water to ½" from top
of cup. Fill with Half-
and-Half. Splash with
Cherry Syrup.

 **PRINCESS CREAM
SODA**

Over Ice, Pour 2 oz
Apricot Syrup. Add
3 oz Soda Water. Fill
with Half-and-Half.
Top with Whipped
Cream.

 **PUERTO APPLE
CREAM SODA**

Over Ice, Pour ¾ oz
Apple Syrup, ¼ oz
Lime Syrup, ½ oz each
Syrup: Rum, Almond.
Add Soda Water to ½"
from top of cup. Fill
with Half-and-Half.

**PUMPKIN LATTE**

Place 1 tablespoon of
Pumpkin based mix in
a cup. Add Espresso.
Stir. Fill with Foamed/
Steamed Milk. Splash
with Praline Syrup.

 **PURPLE CLOUD
COOLER**

Over Ice, Pour 1½ oz
Grape Syrup, ½ oz
Almond Syrup. Fill
with Soda Water.

 **PURPLE COW**

Over Ice, Pour 1½ oz
Grape Syrup, ½ oz
Banana Syrup. Add
Soda Water to ¾" from
top of cup. Fill with
Half-and-Half. Top
with Whipped Cream.
Splash with Grape
Syrup.

 **PURPLE HAZE
COOLER**

Over Ice, Pour 1⅓ oz
Creme de Cassis Syrup,
⅔ oz Creme de Cacao
Syrup. Fill with Soda
Water.

# R

 **PURPLE PASSION**
Over Ice, Pour 1½ oz Grape Syrup. Add ¼ oz each Syrup: Lemon, Pineapple. Fill with Soda Water. Splash with Creme de Cassis Syrup.

 **PURPLE PASSION COOLER**
Over Ice, Pour Grapefruit Juice to 1" from top of cup. Add 2 oz Soda Water. Top with ¾ oz Grape Syrup.

 **QUAD TALL WHIPLESS FOAMLESS**
A tall mocha with 4 shots of espresso, all steamed milk, and no foamed milk or whipped cream.

 **R & R SODA**
Over Ice, Pour 1 oz each Syrup: Rum, Raspberry. Fill with Soda Water.

 **RACEHORSE**
A latte made with 5 shots of espresso in a 16 oz cup.

 **RAMBLING ROSE**
Over Ice, Pour ⅓ oz each Syrup: Strawberry, Raspberry, Lime. Add Ginger Ale to ½" from top of cup. Fill with Soda Water.

 **RASPBERRY BANANA COOLER**
Over Ice, Pour 1 oz each Syrup: Raspberry, Banana. Fill with Soda Water.

 **RASPBERRY BRANDY LATTE**
Pour ¾ oz Raspberry Syrup, ¼ oz Amaretto Syrup. Add Espresso. Fill with Foamed/ Steamed Milk.

 **RASPBERRY COFFEE LATTE**
Pour ½ oz Raspberry Syrup, ¼ oz Coffee Syrup. Add Espresso. Fill with Foamed/ Steamed Milk.

# R

**RASPBERRY CREAM**
Over Ice, Pour 1½ oz
Raspberry Syrup, ½ oz
Creme de Cacao Syrup.
Fill with Half-and-
Half. Top with
Whipped Cream and
Splash of Raspberry
Syrup.

**RASPBERRY DAISY**
Over Ice, Pour 1½ oz
Raspberry Syrup, ½ oz
Lemon Syrup. Fill with
Soda Water.

**RASPBERRY
LICORICE COFFEE
CREAM SODA**
Over Ice, Pour ⅔ oz
each Syrup: Raspberry,
Licorice, Coffee. Fill
with Soda Water to ½"
from top of cup. Top
with Half-and-Half and
Whipped Cream.

**RASPBERRY
MOCHA**

Pour ¾ oz Thick
Chocolate Syrup, ½ oz
Raspberry Syrup. Add
Espresso. Stir. Fill with
Foamed/Steamed Milk.
Top with Whipped
Cream and Chocolate
Sprinkles.

**RASPBERRY
MOCHA CREAM
SODA**

Over Ice, Pour 1 oz
each Syrup: Raspberry,
Creme de Cacao. Add
Soda Water to ½" from
top of cup. Fill with
Half-and-Half. Top
with Whipped Cream.

**RASPBERRY
MOCHA SODA**

Over Ice, Pour 1¼ oz
Raspberry Syrup, ¾ oz
Creme de Cacao Syrup.
Fill with Soda Water.

# R

### RASPBERRY MOCHA STEAMER

Pour ⅔ oz Raspberry Syrup, ⅓ oz Creme de Cacao Syrup. Fill with Foamed/Steamed Milk. Top with Whipped Cream and dust with Chocolate Powder.

### RASPBERRY NUT MOCHA

Pour ½ oz Thick Chocolate Syrup, ¼ oz each Syrup: Raspberry, Almond. Add Espresso. Stir. Fill with Foamed/ Steamed Milk. Top with Whipped Cream. Splash with Raspberry Syrup.

### RASPBERRY RICKEY

Over Ice, Pour 1¼ oz Raspberry Syrup, ¾ oz Lime Syrup. Fill with Soda Water. Splash with Lime Syrup.

### RASPBERRY SODA

Over Ice, Pour 1¾ oz Raspberry Syrup, ¼ oz Vanilla Syrup. Fill with Soda Water.

### RASPBERRY SOUR CREAM PIE CREAM SODA

Over Ice, Pour 1¼ oz Raspberry Syrup, ¾ oz Lemon Syrup. Add 3 oz Soda Water. Fill with Half-and-Half and top with Whipped Cream.

### RASPBERRY TORTE BREVÉ

Pour ½ oz each Syrup: Raspberry, Chocolate. Add Espresso. Fill with Foamed/Steamed Half-and-Half. Top with Whipped Cream. Dust with Chocolate Sprinkles.

### RASPBERRY TRUFFLE LATTE

Pour ¾ oz Thick Chocolate Syrup, ½ oz Raspberry Syrup. Add Espresso. Stir. Fill with Foamed/Steamed Milk. Top with Chocolate Sprinkles and splash with Raspberry Syrup.

# R

## RASPBERRY VANILLA CREAM SODA

Over Ice, Pour 1 oz each Syrup: Raspberry, Vanilla. Add Soda Water to ½ oz from top of cup. Fill with Half-and-Half. Splash with Raspberry Syrup.

## RAZZ-MA-TAZZ

Pour ½ oz each Syrup: Chocolate, Raspberry. Add Espresso. Fill with Foamed/Steamed Milk.

## RED APPLE CREAM SODA

Over Ice, Pour 1 oz Apple Syrup, ¼ oz Cinnamon Syrup, ¾ oz Raspberry Syrup. Add Soda Water to ½" from top of cup. Fill with Half-and-Half.

## RED CLOUD SODA

Over Ice, Pour 1 oz Apricot Syrup, ¼ oz Lemon Syrup, ¾ oz Strawberry Syrup. Fill with Soda Water. Splash with Strawberry Syrup.

## RED DAWN COOLER

Over Ice, Pour 1 oz each Syrup: Cherry, Grape. Fill with Soda Water.

## RED DEVIL

Over Ice, Pour 1¾ oz Cherry Syrup. Fill to ¼" from top of cup with Soda Water. Top with ¼ oz Cinnamon Syrup.

## RED DEVIL SODA

Over Ice, Pour 1¼ oz Cherry Syrup, ¾ oz Cinnamon Syrup. Fill with Soda Water.

## RED LICORICE LATTE

Pour ½ oz each Syrup: Licorice, Raspberry. Add Espresso. Fill with Foamed/Steamed Milk. Splash with Raspberry Syrup.

# R

### RED SLED

Over Ice, Pour 1 oz each Syrup: Peach, Cranberry. Add Soda Water to ½" from top of cup. Fill with Half-and-Half.

### RICH'S HONEY BEE LATTE

Pour ½ oz Honey, ¼ oz any flavor Syrup. Add Espresso. Stir. Fill with Foamed/Steamed Milk.

### RICO BREVÉ

Pour ¾ oz Cinnamon Syrup, ¼ oz Orange Syrup. Add Espresso. Fill with Foamed/Steamed Half-and-Half.

### RISTRETTO (Short Pour)

Pour ¾-1 oz Water through a Single Measure of Coffee— 7 grams.

### RICHLAND BOMBER

Pour ¾ oz B-52 Syrup, ¼ oz Cherry Syrup. Add a triple shot Ristretto. Top with Foamed/Steamed Half-and-Half. Garnish with a Maraschino Cherry.

### ROCKET

Pour a double shot of Espresso. Add Ice. Add Soda Water to ½ full. Fill with Milk. Top with Whipped Cream.

### ROCKY ROAD

Pour ½ oz of each Thick Syrup: Chocolate, Marshmallow. Add ¼ oz Almond Syrup. Add Espresso. Stir. Fill with Foamed/Steamed Milk. Top with Whipped Cream and Chocolate Sprinkles.

### ROOT BEER FLOAT

Over Ice, Pour 2 oz Root Beer Syrup. Add 3 oz Soda Water. Top with Half-and-Half and Whipped Cream.

# R

## ROSE'S RUBY HEART

Over Ice, Pour 1¾ oz Strawberry Syrup, ¼ oz Lime Syrup. Add Soda Water to ½" from top of cup. Top with Half-and-Half.

## ROSEY O'TOOLE

Over Ice, Pour 1 oz each Syrup: Irish Cream, Strawberry. Add 2 oz Soda Water. Top with Half-and-Half. Splash with Creme de Menthe Syrup.

## ROSY PIPPIN

Over Ice, Pour ½ oz Apple Syrup, ¼ oz Lemon Syrup. Add 3 oz Soda Water. Fill with Ginger Ale. Splash with Grenadine Syrup.

## ROYAL STREET COFFEE

Pour ½ oz Amaretto Syrup, ⅓ oz Creme de Cacao Syrup. Add Hot Water to 1" from top of cup. Top with Espresso and Whipped Cream.

## RUBY FIZZ

Over Ice, Pour 1½ oz Raspberry Syrup, ½ oz Blackberry Syrup. Fill with Soda Water. Splash with Lemon Syrup.

## RUM ALEXANDER

Over Ice, Pour 1¼ oz Rum Syrup, ¾ oz Creme de Cacao Syrup. Top with 3 oz Half-and-Half. Dust with Powdered Nutmeg.

## RUM AND COCONUT COOLER

Over Ice, Pour 1 oz each Syrup: Rum, Coconut. Fill with Soda Water.

# R

## RUM AND PINEAPPLE COOLER

Over Ice, Pour 1 oz each Syrup: Rum, Pineapple. Fill with Soda Water.

## RUM COFFEE SODA

Over Ice, Pour 1 oz each Syrup: Rum, Coffee. Add Half-and-Half to 1" from top of cup. Fill with Soda Water.

## RUM SCREWDRIVER

Over Ice, Pour ¾ oz Rum Syrup. Fill with Orange Juice.

## RUMETTO

Pour ½ oz each Syrup: Rum, Amaretto. Add Espresso. Fill with Foamed/Steamed Milk.

## SAINT PATRICK'S DAY MOCHA JAVA

Pour ¾ oz Thick Chocolate Syrup, ½ oz Irish Cream Syrup. Add Espresso. Stir. Fill with Foamed/Steamed Milk. Top with Whipped Cream and Splash with Irish Cream Syrup.

## SAMBUCA COFFEE COOLER

Over Ice, Pour ¾ oz each Syrup: Coffee, Sambuca. Fill with Soda Water. Top with Whipped Cream and 3 Dark Roasted Coffee Beans.

## SAN JUAN SLING

Over Ice, Pour ¾ oz each Syrup: Rum, Cherry. Add ½ oz Lime Syrup. Fill with Soda Water. Splash with Lime Syrup.

## SANGRIA SPRITZER

Over Ice, Pour ¾ oz each Syrup: Orange, Creme de Cassis. Add ½ oz Lime Syrup. Fill with Soda Water.

# S

 **SARATOGA COOLER**

Over Ice, Pour 1 oz Lemon Syrup. Fill with Ginger Ale.

 **SAVORY LIME COOLER**

Over Ice, Pour 2 oz Lime Syrup. Fill with Soda Water. Splash with Lime Syrup.

 **SCORPION**

Over Ice, Pour 1 oz Orange Syrup, ¾ oz Lemon Syrup, ¼ oz Pineapple Syrup. Fill with Soda Water.

 **SEA BREEZE**

Over Ice, Pour 4 oz Grapefruit Juice. Add Soda Water to ¼" from top of cup. Top with ½ oz of Cranberry Syrup.

 **SHADY LADY**

Over Ice, Fill with Grapefruit Juice to ½" from top of cup. Top with ½ oz Melon Syrup. Splash with Soda Water.

 **SHANGHAI COOLER**

Over Ice, Pour ⅔ oz each Syrup: Anisette, Lemon, Rum. Fill with Soda Water.

 **SHIRLEY TEMPLE**

Over Ice, Pour 1 oz Grenadine Syrup. Fill with Ginger Ale. Stir.

 **SHORT "A" WITH ROOM**

An 8 oz Americano with room for cream.

 **SHORT SINGLE**

A latte or an Americano in a short cup.

 **SIESTA SLING**

Over Ice, Pour ⅔ oz each Syrup: Apricot, Banana, Coconut. Fill with Soda Water. Splash with Lime Syrup.

 **SILK BREVÉ**

Pour ½ oz Honey, ¼ oz Anisette Syrup. Add Espresso. Stir. Fill with Foamed/Steamed Half-and-Half.

# S

### SINGAPORE SLING COOLER

Over Ice, Pour ⅔ oz each Syrup: Almond, Grenadine, Orange. Fill with Soda Water. Stir.

### SINGLE

A single shot of Espresso.

### SKINNY SLEEPER

A latte made with decaf coffee and nonfat milk.

### SKINNY TALLMOND

An almond latte, made with a double shot of espresso, nonfat steamed milk, no foam, in a tall cup.

### SMITH & KERNS

Over Ice, Pour 1⅓ oz Coffee Syrup, ⅔ oz Creme de Cacao Syrup, 1½ oz Half-and-Half, 2 oz Soda Water. Stir gently.

### SMITH & WESSON

Over Ice, Pour 1⅓ oz Coffee Syrup, ⅔ oz Creme de Cacao Syrup, 1½ oz Half-and-Half, 2 oz Cola. Stir gently.

### SNICKERS

Pour ⅓ oz each Thick Syrup: Chocolate, Caramel. Add ⅓ oz Hazelnut Syrup. Add Espresso. Stir. Fill with Foamed/Steamed Milk. Top with Whipped Cream and garnish with threads of Thick Caramel Syrup.

### SNOW CAP

Pour 1 oz Vanilla Syrup. Fill with Foamed/Steamed Milk. Top with Whipped Cream and dust with Vanilla Powder and/or White Chocolate Powder.

### SOLO

A single shot of Espresso.

# S

 **SOLOMON'S SODA**
Over Ice, Pour 1 oz each Syrup: Apricot, Creme de Cassis. Fill with Soda Water.

 **SOUTH OF THE BORDER**
Over Ice, Pour 1¼ oz Coffee Syrup, ¾ oz Orange Syrup. Fill with Soda Water.

 **SOY MILK LATTE**
Pour Espresso. Fill with Foamed/Steamed Soy Milk.

 **SPANISH EYES**
Pour ⅓ oz each Syrup: Creme de Cacao, Rum. Fill with Hot Water to 1" from top of cup. Add a double shot of Espresso. Top with Whipped Cream. Splash with Creme de Cacao Syrup.

 **SPARKLING CITRUS COOLER**
Over Ice, Pour 1 oz Lime Syrup. Add 4 oz Grapefruit Juice. Fill with Soda Water.

 **SPARKLING ROSY SODA**
Over Ice, Pour 1¼ oz Apple Syrup, ¾ oz Strawberry Syrup. Fill with Soda Water.

 **SPICED & ICED COFFEE**
Pour ½ oz Simple Syrup. Add Espresso. Add a Pinch of Cinnamon and Nutmeg Powder. Stir. Add Ice. Fill with Cold Water.

 **SPICED RUM COFFEE**
Pour ⅓ oz each Syrup: Rum, Cinnamon. Fill with Hot Water to 1" from top of cup. Add Espresso.

 **SPICED TEA SODA**
Over Ice, Pour 1 oz each Syrup: Cinnamon, Lemon. Add ½ oz Orange Syrup. Fill with Soda Water.

# S

###  SPICY CINNAMON MOCHA

Pour 1 oz Thick Chocolate Syrup, ⅓ oz Cinnamon Syrup. Add Espresso. Stir. Fill with Foamed/Steamed Milk. Top with Whipped Cream and Chocolate Sprinkles.

###  SPICY CRANBERRY LEMON SODA

Over Ice, Pour ⅔ oz each Syrup: Cranberry, Lemon. Add ½ oz Cinnamon Syrup. Fill with Soda Water.

###  SPICY ICED ESPRESSO

Pour 1 oz Cinnamon Syrup. Add Espresso. Fill with Ice. Add Cold Water to top of cup. Splash with Lemon Syrup.

### SPICY LICORICE LATTE

Pour ⅓ oz each Syrup: Licorice, Orange, Cinnamon. Add Espresso. Fill with Foamed/Steamed Milk. Dust with Cinnamon Powder.

### SPICY PEACH LATTE

Pour ½ oz Peach Syrup, ¼ oz Cinnamon Syrup. Add Espresso. Fill with Foamed/Steamed Milk.

###  SPUMONI COFFEE

Pour ¼ oz each Syrup: Cinnamon, Creme de Cacao, Orange, Almond. Fill with Hot Water to 1" from top of cup. Top with Espresso and Whipped Cream.

### STEAMBOAT SPRINGS CREAM SODA

Over Ice, Pour 1 oz each Syrup: Licorice, Blueberry. Add 2 oz Soda Water. Fill with Half-and-Half. Top with Whipped Cream.

### STEAMER

Pour 1 oz any Flavored Syrup. Fill with Foamed/Steamed Milk. Top with Whipped Cream.

# S

 **STRAWBERRY ANGEL**

Over Ice, Pour 1½ oz Strawberry Syrup, ½ oz Coconut Syrup. Add Soda Water to ½" from top of cup. Fill with Half-and-Half. Top with Whipped Cream.

 **STRAWBERRY APPLE LATTE**

Pour ½ oz each Syrup: Strawberry, Apple. Add Espresso. Fill with Foamed/Steamed Milk.

 **STRAWBERRY BANANA COOLER**

Over Ice, Pour 1 oz each Syrup: Strawberry, Banana. Fill with Soda Water.

 **STRAWBERRY BANANA MILK**

Over Ice, Pour ¾ oz each Syrup: Strawberry, Banana. Fill with Cold Milk. Splash with Vanilla Syrup.

 **STRAWBERRY BLOND**

Over Ice, Pour 1⅓ oz Strawberry Syrup. Fill with Soda Water to ¼" from top. Top with ⅔ oz Lemon Syrup.

 **STRAWBERRY CRANBERRY FROST**

Over Ice, Pour 1 oz each Syrup: Strawberry, Cranberry. Fill with Soda Water. Splash with Strawberry Syrup.

 **STRAWBERRY CREAM SODA**

Over Ice, Pour 1 oz each Syrup: Strawberry, Vanilla. Add Soda Water to ½" from top of cup. Top with Half-and-Half.

 **STRAWBERRY CRUSH**

Over Ice, Pour 1½ oz Strawberry Syrup. Fill with Soda Water to ¼" from top of cup. Top with ½ oz Orange Syrup.

# S

 **STRAWBERRY DAWN**

Over Ice, Pour 1¼ oz Strawberry Syrup, ¾ oz Coconut Syrup. Add Soda Water to ½" from top of cup. Fill with Half-and-Half. Splash with Strawberry Syrup.

 **STRAWBERRY LICORICE LATTE**

Pour ½ oz Strawberry Syrup, ¼ oz Licorice Syrup. Add Espresso. Fill with Foamed/ Steamed Milk.

 **STRAWBERRY MARGARITA**

Over Ice, Pour 1⅓ oz Strawberry Syrup, ⅓ oz each Syrup: Orange, Lime. Fill with Soda Water.

 **STRAWBERRY NEWTON CREAM SODA**

Over Ice, Pour ⅔ oz each Syrup: Strawberry, Apple, Pineapple. Add Soda Water to ½" from top of cup. Fill with Half-and-Half.

 **STRAWBERRY PINEAPPLE CREAM SODA**

Over Ice, Pour ¾ oz each Syrup: Strawberry, Pineapple. Add ½ oz Vanilla Syrup. Add Soda Water to ½" from top of cup. Top with Half-and-Half.

 **STRAWBERRY SHORTCAKE CREAM SODA**

Over Ice, Pour 1¼ oz Strawberry Syrup, ½ oz Almond Syrup, ¼ oz Creme de Cacao Syrup. Add Soda Water to ½" from top of cup. Fill with Half-and-Half and top with Whipped Cream.

 **STRAWBERRY SLIM**

Over Ice, Pour 2 oz Strawberry Syrup. Add Soda Water to ½" from top of cup. Top with Nonfat Milk.

# S

 **STRAWBERRY SUNRISE**

Over Ice, Pour 1 oz Strawberry Syrup. Add Orange Juice to ½" from top of cup. Fill with Soda Water.

 **STRAWBERRY VANILLA CREAM SODA**

Over Ice, Pour 1 oz each Syrup: Strawberry, Vanilla. Add Soda Water to ½" from top of cup. Fill with Half-and-Half. Splash with Strawberry Syrup.

 **STRAWBERRIES AND CREAM**

Over Ice, Pour 1½ oz Strawberry Syrup. Fill with Cold Milk or Half-and-Half. Splash with Strawberry Syrup.

 **SUGAR DADDY LATTE**

Pour ⅔ oz Thick Caramel Syrup, ½ oz Hazelnut Syrup. Add Espresso. Stir. Fill with Foamed/Steamed Milk.

 **SUMMER CYCLIST**

Over Ice, Pour ½ oz each Syrup: Strawberry, Lime, Orange, and Grape. Fill with Soda Water.

 **SUN SODA**

Over Ice, Pour 2 oz Orange Syrup. Add Half-and-Half to ½" from top of cup. Top with Ginger Ale or Soda Water.

 **SUNBURST**

Pour ½ oz each Syrup: Chocolate, Orange. Add Espresso. Fill with Foamed/Steamed Milk.

 **SUNRISE SODA 1**

Over Ice, Pour 1 oz each Syrup: Orange, Pineapple. Fill with Soda Water. Splash with Grenadine Syrup.

 **SUNRISE SODA 2**

Over Ice, Pour 1¾ oz Orange Syrup, ¼ oz Grenadine Syrup. Fill with Soda Water.

# S

 **SUNSET COOLER**
Over Ice, Pour ½ oz
Grenadine Syrup, 1 oz
Orange Syrup, ½ oz
Pineapple Syrup. Fill
with Soda Water.

 **SUNSET SODA**
Over Ice, Pour ⅔ oz
each Syrup: Peach,
Raspberry, Pineapple.
Fill with Soda Water.

 **SUNSET STRIP
SODA**
Over Ice, Pour 1 oz
Mandarino Syrup. Fill
with equal parts of
Ginger Ale and Soda
Water. Splash with
Grenadine Syrup.

 **SWAMP WATER**
Over Ice, Pour 1 oz
each Syrup: Orange,
Root Beer. Fill with
Soda Water.

 **SWEET & SOUR
SODA**
Over Ice, Pour 1 oz
Apple Syrup. Add Soda
Water to 1" from top of
cup. Fill with
Grapefruit Juice. Splash
with Cherry Syrup.

 **TAHITI CLUB
COOLER**
Over Ice, Pour 1 oz
Rum Syrup, ⅓ oz each
Syrup: Lemon, Lime,
Pineapple. Fill with
Soda Water. Splash
with Maraschino
Syrup.

 **TAHITIAN
CARAMEL CREAM
SODA**
Over Ice, Pour ½ oz
each Syrup: Coconut,
Praline, Pineapple,
Caramel. Fill with Soda
Water to ½" from top
of cup. Fill with Half-
and-Half.

 **TAHITIAN COFFEE**
Pour ¾ oz Coconut
Syrup. Add 4 oz Hot
Water. Add Espresso.
Top with Whipped
Cream. Dust with
Chocolate Powder.

 **TALL "A" BLACK**
Tall Americano with no
cream.

# T

 **TALL SKINNY LATTE**
A tall latte made with nonfat milk.

 **TALL TOO**
A tall latte made with 2% milk.

 **TALL WHIPLESS FOAMLESS**
A tall mocha with all steamed milk and no foamed milk or whipped cream.

 **TANGERINE AND LIME SODA**
Over Ice, Pour 1 oz each Syrup: Tangerine, Lime. Fill with Soda Water. Splash with Lime Syrup.

 **TANGERINE CHERRY SODA**
Over Ice, Pour 1¼ oz Mandarino Syrup, ¾ oz Cherry Syrup. Fill with Soda Water.

 **TEQUILA SUNSET**
Over Ice, Fill to ¼" from top of cup with Orange Juice. Top with ¼ oz Grenadine Syrup.

 **TERESA'S TROPICAL COOLER**
Over Ice, Pour ½ oz each Syrup: Pineapple, Mango, Orange, Coconut. Fill with Soda Water. Splash with Lemon Syrup.

 **THAI ICED COFFEE**
Pour a double shot of Espresso. Add Ice. Fill with Sweetened Condensed Milk.

 **THRILLER**
Over Ice, Pour ⅓ oz each Syrup: Grenadine, Orange, Pineapple. Add 1 oz Strawberry Syrup. Add Soda Water to ½" from top of cup. Top with 2 oz Half-and-Half.

 **THUNDER THIGHS**
A double tall mocha made with whole milk and topped with extra whipped cream.

# T

### TOASTED ALMOND

Pour ⅔ oz Amaretto Syrup, ¼ oz Almond Syrup. Add Espresso. Fill with Foamed/ Steamed Milk. Top with Whipped Cream.

### TOASTED COCONUT CREAM BREVÉ

Pour ⅔ oz Coconut Syrup, ¼ oz Hazelnut Syrup. Add Espresso. Fill with Foamed/ Steamed Half-and-Half and top with Whipped Cream.

### TREE TOP CREAM SODA

Over Ice, Pour 1 oz each Syrup: Apple, Apricot. Add Soda Water to ½" from top of cup. Fill with Half-and-Half.

### TRIPLE SQUEEZE SODA

Over Ice, Pour ⅔ oz each Syrup: Lime, Mandarino, Orange. Fill with Soda Water.

### TRIPLE TALL ICED SKINNY WITH VANILLA

A nonfat milk iced latte with 3 shots of espresso and vanilla syrup.

### TRIPLE TALL WHIPLESS

A mocha with a triple shot of espresso and no whipped cream, in a tall cup.

### TRIPLE TALL WHIPLESS BILLIARD BALL

A mocha with a triple shot of espresso, no foam, no whipped cream, in a tall cup.

### TROPICAL COFFEE COOLER

Pour Espresso. Add Ice. Add ½ oz each Syrup: Mango, Pineapple. Fill with Milk.

### TROPICAL HEART

Pour ⅓ oz Passion Fruit Syrup into a steaming pitcher, add Apple Cider. Steam and serve.

# T

 **TROPICAL
COCONUT SODA**

Over Ice, Pour 1½ oz
Coconut Syrup, ½ oz
Mango Syrup. Fill with
Soda Water. Splash
with Lime Syrup.

 **TROPICAL
GRAPEFRUIT NOG**

Over Ice, Pour 1 oz
Mango Syrup, 3 oz
Grapefruit Juice. Fill
with Egg Nog. Dust
with Nutmeg.

 **TROPICAL LATTE**

Pour ½ oz each Syrup:
Coconut, Pineapple.
Add Espresso. Fill with
Foamed/Steamed Milk.

**TROPICAL
PINEAPPLE SODA**

Over Ice, Pour 1¼ oz
Pineapple Syrup, ½ oz
Amaretto Syrup, ¼ oz
Rum Syrup. Fill with
Soda Water.

 **TROPICAL TEASE**

Over Ice, Pour ⅔ oz
each Syrup: Passion
Fruit, Banana,
Coconut. Fill with
Soda Water.

 **TURKISH COFFEE**

Pour 3 oz Hot Water.
Add 1 tablespoon
Equal. Stir. Add a
double shot Espresso.
Splash a few drops of
Rose Water (optional).

 **TURKISH COFFEE
COLA SODA**

Pour a double shot of
Espresso. Add Ice. Fill
with Cola to ½" from
top of cup. Top with
Half-and-Half.

 **TURTLE SUNDAE**

Pour ¾ oz Thick
Chocolate Syrup, ⅓ oz
each Syrup: Caramel,
Praline. Add Espresso.
Stir. Fill with Foamed/
Steamed Half-and-
Half. Top with
Whipped Cream.

 **TUTTI FRUTTI**

Over Ice, Pour ½ oz
each Syrup: Maraschino,
Amaretto, Apple,
Peach. Fill with Soda
Water. Splash with
Maraschino Syrup.

# T

 **TUSCANY**

Pour ¾ oz Thick Chocolate Syrup, ⅓ oz Orange Syrup. Add Espresso. Stir. Fill with Foamed/Steamed Milk. Top with Whipped Cream and Chocolate Sprinkles.

**UNFUZZY NAVEL**

Over Ice, Pour 1¼ oz Orange Syrup, ½ oz Peach Syrup, ¼ oz Lemon Syrup. Fill with Soda Water. Splash with Grenadine Syrup.

 **VANILLA FUN CAPPUCCINO**

Pour ¾ oz Vanilla Syrup into steaming pitcher. Fill pitcher ⅓ full with Cold Milk. Foam and steam Milk-Syrup mixture. Set pitcher aside. Pour Espresso. Allow flavored Steamed Milk to pour under Foam to ½" from top of cup. Top with 2" "cap" of dense, flavored Foam.

**VANILLA COFFEE LATTE**

Pour ½ oz each Syrup: Vanilla, Coffee. Add Espresso. Fill with Foamed/Steamed Milk.

 **VANILLA MOCHA LATTE**

Pour ½ oz Thick Chocolate Syrup, ½ oz Vanilla Syrup. Add Espresso. Stir. Fill with Foamed/Steamed Milk.

**VERY BERRY ITALIAN SODA**

Over Ice, Pour 1 oz each Syrup: Raspberry, Boysenberry. Fill with Soda Water.

 **VERY BERRY ROYAL SODA**

Over Ice, Pour ⅔ oz each Syrup: Blackberry, Raspberry, Strawberry. Add Soda Water to ½" from top of cup. Fill with Half-and-Half. Top with Whipped Cream.

# V

## VIENNA MELANGE
In an 8 oz cup, Pour ½ oz Irish Cream Syrup, ¼ oz Orange Syrup. Add Espresso. Top with Whipped Cream.

## VIENNESE CAFE MOCHA
A mocha with ½ oz of cinnamon syrup added.

## VIENNESE COFFEE
Pour ½ oz Vanilla Syrup. Add 3 oz Hot Water and a double shot of Espresso. Top with Whipped Cream. Dust with Cinnamon or Nutmeg.

## VIENNESE MOCHA
Pour ⅔ oz Thick Chocolate Syrup, ¼ oz each Syrup: Cinnamon, Almond. Add Espresso. Stir. Fill with Foamed/ Steamed Milk. Top with Whipped Cream. Garnish with threads of thick Chocolate Syrup over Whipped Cream.

## VIETNAMESE COFFEE
Pour Espresso. Add Ice. Fill with Sweetened Condensed Milk.

## VINNY'S CAPPUCCINO
Pour ¾ oz Chocolate Mint Syrup, ¼ oz Cinnamon Syrup. Foam and Steam Milk. Set pitcher aside. Pour Espresso. Allow Steamed Milk to pour under Foam to ½" from top of cup. Top with 2" "cap" of dense Foam. Dust with Chocolate Powder.

## WEST INDIAN COOLER
Over Ice, Pour ½ oz each Syrup: Orange, Pineapple, Banana, Rum. Fill with Soda Water. Splash with Lime Syrup. Dust with Nutmeg Powder.

# Z

 **WET CAPPUCCINO**
First Foam and Steam
Milk. Set pitcher aside.
Pour Espresso. Allow
Steamed Milk to pour
under Foam to ¼" from
top of cup. Top with a
short "cap" of dense
Foam. Dust with
Chocolate Powder or
Nutmeg.

 **WETZLAR COFFEE**
Pour a double shot of
Espresso. Add Ice. Pour
¾ oz each Syrup:
Cherry, Creme de
Cacao. Fill with Cold
Milk or Half-and-Half.

 **WHITE CLOUD**
Over Ice, Pour 2 oz
Anisette Syrup. Fill
with Soda Water.
Splash with Vanilla
Syrup.

**WHITE COW**
Pour ¾ oz Thick
Chocolate Syrup, ½ oz
Vanilla Syrup. Add
Espresso. Stir. Fill with
Foamed/Steamed Milk.
Top with Whipped
Cream and Chocolate
Sprinkles.

**WHY BOTHER?**
A latte made with decaf
coffee and nonfat milk.

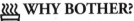 **WOO WOO**
Over Ice, Pour 1 oz
each Syrup: Peach,
Cranberry. Fill with
Soda Water.

**YANKEE DOG
WITH A WHITE
HAT ON A LEASH**

Fill to ½" from top
with Hot Water. Add
Espresso. Top with Hot
Milk Foam. To Go.

 **YELLOWBIRD**
Over Ice, Pour ½ oz
each Syrup: Pineapple,
Banana, Lemon, Rum.
Fill with Soda Water.

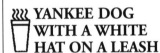 **ZOMBIE**
Over Ice, Pour ½ oz
Creme de Cacao Syrup.
Add ¼ oz each Syrup:
Strawberry, Vanilla,
Pineapple, Orange,
Lime. Fill with Soda
Water.

**Chapter 3**

# Coffee & Espresso: Past to Present

The Evolution of Coffee:

1. It was first eaten as food: the berries were mixed with fat and rolled into balls to carry on long journeys.

2. It was also drunk as a fermented wine.

3. It was then taken as a medicine.

4. Finally, it was roasted and brewed as a beverage.

 Nomadic tribes preserved the coffee cherries to transport them long distances.

 Coffee has been in existence at least as long as man.

 The first coffee tree was discovered growing wild in Ethiopia, Africa. It was a species of the Arabica plant.

The most widely accepted legend associated with the discovery of coffee concerns a goatherder named Kaldi of Ethiopia. Around the year 600 A.D., Kaldi was amazed as he noticed his goats behaving in a frisky manner after eating the leaves and berries of a coffee shrub. Of course, he had to try them.

---

The coffee plant was first cultivated in Yemen in the seventh century.

---

The Arabs are generally believed to be the first to brew coffee.

---

The word *coffee* likely derives from the root meaning of the Arabic word *gahwa*, a word which may be translated as "wine" or as "excitement."

---

Coffee was first known in Europe as Arabian Wine.

---

Around the year 950 A.D., Arabs soaked green coffee beans in cold water to make the first coffee beverage.

---

Shortly before the year 1000 A.D., coffee frequently was administered as a medicine.

Roasted coffee goes back to the 13th century when people began roasting the beans before brewing them. Beans were generally roasted in a heavy pan over a charcoal fire before whole beans were boiled.

After the Arabs learned to boil water, they used green coffee beans to make their brew.

Turkey began to roast the coffee bean in the 13th century, and some 300 years later in the 1500s the country had become the chief distributor of coffee with markets established in Egypt, Syria, Persia, and Venice, Italy.

Late in the 1300s Arabs discovered the process of roasting coffee.

In the 14th century Arabs started to cultivate coffee plants. The first commercially grown and harvested coffee originated on the Arabian Peninsula near the port of Mocha.

In the early 1400s alcohol was forbidden by the Koran, and coffee soon became the replacement beverage. It was drunk both at home and at coffee-houses.

A four-verse poem to coffee, one of the first, was written in Mecca in 1511.

It is thought that the first roasted, *ground* coffee was probably brewed in Syria in the 1520s. Roasted beans were pounded to a powder with a mortar and pestle before being thrown into boiling water. The brew was consumed grounds and all.

Finely ground coffee beans boiled in water is still known as "Turkish coffee." Coffee is still made this way today in Turkey and Greece or anywhere else Turkish coffee is served.

In 1554 in Constantinople, two coffeehouses opened. They did very well. Soon there were many.

In 1586 Sassafras tea was about as popular as espresso is now. Sassafras stands could be found throughout London. The first large shipments from North America were Sassafras roots to quench the ever increasing demand. The tea stands vanished virtually overnight, however, when rumor spread that the New World Indians drank Sassafras broth to treat syphilis.

By 1600 A.D. coffee drinking had come to the Orient and soon became very popular.

The Venetians first introduced coffee to Europe in 1615.

Some experts believe that sugar as a coffee sweetener stimulated the rapid growth of coffee in Europe. As coffee was introduced into each European country, sugar was introduced with it.

The year was 1632: early European coffeehouses quickly became centers of social activities and culture.

Coffeehouses of the late 1600s frequently hired live entertainment: singers, flute and violin players to amuse the clientele.

Many of these early day coffeehouses were known as "penny universities." They charged a penny for admission and a cup of coffee. You could then participate in the intellectual discussions of the time, all stimulated by the fresh-brewed coffee.

Coffeehouses not only served as "Penny Universities," but as "Penny Post Offices." In 1863 several coffeehouses in London collected mail and provided private boxes—before the government got involved. The king laid claim as a royal prerogative, and taxes were collected. Soon there were no longer "Penny Post Offices."

Lloyd's of London began as Edward Lloyd's coffeehouse.

It was during the 1600s that the first coffee mill made its debut in London.

Coffee was first introduced in America as a consumer good in 1660. It was sold to the affluent Dutch of New Amsterdam. The English soon conquered New Amsterdam and renamed it New York.

In 1645 a cafe in Venice began serving beverages made from water and ice as well as roasted coffee. By 1761 Venice had become the coffee capital of Italy with one coffee shop for every 500 inhabitants.

Coffee as a medicine reached its highest and lowest point in the 1600s in England. Wild medical contraptions were used to treat the sick by administering a mixture of coffee and an assortment of heated butter, honey, and oil.

In 1670 Dorothy Jones of Boston was granted a license to sell coffee and so became the first American coffee trader.

William Penn purchased a pound of coffee in New York in 1683 for $4.68.

One pound of coffee in New York was worth as much as four acres of land. The year was 1683.

Milk as an additive to coffee became popular in the 1680s when a French physician recommended that cafe au lait be used for medicinal purposes.

The first Parisian cafe opened in 1689 to serve coffee.

 In 1711 coffee sold at an Amsterdam auction for 47¢ a pound. The commodity price on the world exchanges in 1993 dipped as low as 40¢ a pound. So much for inflation ....

 Adding sugar to coffee is believed to have started in 1715 in the court of King Louis XIV, the French monarch.

 In the book, *Trip Through Happy Arabia,* (1716) a Frenchman included one of the first documentations of the history of coffee.

 Wealthy Turkish homes of the 16th century employed full time coffee stewards.

 By the 1720s coffee shops in Venice offered a wide range of goods and services including iced beverages and newspapers.

 Coffee plants were introduced to the Americas for cultivation in 1723 when a French ship captain persuaded the crown to allow him to take a few small coffee plants back to Martinique.

The year was 1716: Venetian coffee shop merchants began distributing leaflets exalting their new product, coffee. This may be the first example of advertising for coffee shops.

In 1727 seedlings smuggled from Paris became the first coffee plants to be cultivated in Brazil. Brazil is presently by far the world's largest producer of coffee.

Bach wrote a coffee cantata in 1732.

Filtering coffee with metal, paper, and cloth filters began during the 1700s.

Before the first French cafe appeared in the late 1700s, coffee was sold by street vendors in Europe in the Arab fashion. Arabs were the forerunners of today's sidewalk espresso vendors.

In the year 1763 there were over 200 coffee shops in Venice, yet the world's first public restaurant in Paris would not open until 1770.

The heavy tea tax imposed on the colonies in 1773, which caused the "Boston Tea Party," resulted in America switching from tea to coffee. Drinking coffee was an expression of freedom.

During the revolution, the founding fathers of the U.S. formed their national strategies in coffeehouses.

In early America coffee was usually taken between meals and after dinner.

 By 1777 almost 20 million coffee plants were being cultivated on Martinique. That number was sufficient to satisfy three-quarters of Europe's demand.

 In the year 1790 there were two firsts in the United States: the first wholesale coffee roasting company; and the first newspaper advertisement featuring coffee.

 By 1843 coffee had become ingrained in French society, with over 3,000 cafes serving it.

 A Frenchman, Lebrun, invented the first working espresso machine in 1838.

 Frontier lore suggests that Native Americans traded their buffalo hides and other furs to trappers and traders for precious coffee beans.

 The authors of the book *Coffee and Tea* suggest that the site of Fort Laramie "… was swapped for tools, rifles, and a few bags of Java beans."

 The Enterprise Manufacturing Co. of Philadelphia started manufacturing old general store coffee mills in the mid 1800s. Today the large two-wheel counter models are a popular item at antique auctions.

By 1850 the manual coffee grinder had found its way to most upper middle class kitchens of the U.S.

 In 1864 Jabez Burns invented a coffee roaster that did not have to be removed from the fire to discharge the beans. Within ten years, home roasting was virtually obsolete.

 The Civil War in the United States elevated the popularity of coffee to new heights. Soldiers went to war with coffee beans as a primary ration.

 Abraham Lincoln never had anything more than a cup of coffee for breakfast.

 The first espresso coffee machine with steam and water control was invented by Kessel in 1878.

 Caleb Chase and James Sanborn first packaged ground coffee in a sealed tin can. The year was 1878.

 That little turnkey that your parents used for opening coffee cans was patented in 1886. The whoosh sound of air and the seductive aroma of preground coffee beans was a great marketing ploy that sold millions of pounds of product over the next hundred years.

 The year was 1885; the city was Turin, Italy. The first commercial bulk brewing espresso machine was patented.

"Candle auctions" of coffee lots took place on the Coffee and Tea Exchange in London during the late 1880s. A candle was lit, and bids were called. The last bid taken before the candle flickered out was the winner.

The process of roasting coffee using hot air as the only medium was developed about 1885 when the beans were first placed in a chamber heated by natural gas. This method remains today the best and most popular method for roasting coffee.

The vacuum pack, invented in 1898, made it possible to preserve roasted coffee. Preserved coffee, though, not fresh coffee. Ten years later, Hills Brothers Coffee began using this packaging method.

The first electric gear-driven coffee grinder made its appearance in 1900.

By the early 1900s electricity had been merged with the coffee maker. Heating elements were attached to existing stove-top models. However, the very first electric coffeemaker was developed in London in 1881. This crude device featured electric coils encased in an urn. Electric coffeemakers would not achieve popularity for another 20 years.

In 1900 coffee was often delivered door-to-door in the United States by horse-pulled wagons.

*Sans caffeine* is a French phrase meaning "without caffeine." Sanka, the decaffeinated coffee, was packaged in 1903.

---

The first commercial espresso machine was manufactured in Italy in 1906.

---

While dining at the famous Hermitage, the old home of Andrew Jackson in Nashville, Tennessee, Teddy Roosevelt was asked if he wanted more coffee. "Deelighted!" responded Teddy. "It's good to the last drop!" Maxwell House® Coffee's advertising slogan was coined.

---

Espresso is to Italy what champagne is to France.

---

The average age of an Italian barista is 48. A barista is a respected job title in Italy.

---

In Italy coffee and espresso are synonymous.

---

Italians do not drink espresso during meals. Espresso is considered to be a separate event and is given its own time.

---

At a Walgreen's soda fountain during the 1920s, "Pop" Caulson invented the milk shake. Today the Moka shake is a popular request. Simply add a short shot of espresso before blending.

Around 1920 the Coffee table replaced the tea table in American living rooms. From the 17th century until the 1920s most people placed full height (at least 26 inches tall) tea tables in front of their sofas.

 The "coffee break" in the American workplace came about during World War II. Employers found that their employees would work longer and harder if they were supplied with a coffee break during their shifts. U.S. studies shortly thereafter reported that 10,000 marriages a year were directly traceable to romances which began during these coffee breaks.

 The year was 1928: Brazil's economy collapsed owing to the over-production of coffee. By 1931 the National Coffee Department in Brazil had ordered the destruction of surplus stocks.

 The stovetop Moka Express coffee maker popular in Europe was designed in 1933. It took several years to achieve popularity. More than 20 million units have been sold since World War II.

 In the early 1950s the Moka Bar opened in London. It was England's first "Espresso Bar." Many followed. Popular with both teens and adults, these espresso bars served up espresso, cappuccino, poetry, acoustical music, and socializing.

The drug store soda fountain was a popular U.S. neighborhood institution until the mid 1950s when the booming post war cosmetics business became so profitable that floor space was taken over, and Americans soon migrated to the fast food drive-ins for their sodas and beverages.

---

By the 1960s coffeehouses and folk musicians had appeared on the U.S. scene. Usually adjoining university districts in large cities, they seemed to focus their appeal and marketing efforts towards the counter-culture, a far cry from the polished coffee bars of the 1990s.

---

Germany began marketing the Melitta® drip coffeemaker in 1960. Later this vastly improved coffee making method spread to the U.S. and Canada. Drinking recirculated coffee from percolators became a thing of the past.

---

Irish coffee was first served up in the U.S. at the Buena Vista Cafe in San Francisco in 1953. An immediate hit, the drink continues to draw throngs of tourists to the San Francisco water-front to this day.

---

Through trial and error, the then-owner of San Francisco's Buena Vista and the former mayor of that city (a prominent dairy owner) discovered how to make whipped cream float over a hot Irish coffee. The bottom-bent cream was aged 48 hours before being whipped to a precise consistency. It would now float on the hot nectar.

The "Killer Frost" of 1975 in the coffee growing regions of Brazil created a serious shortage of coffee on the international market. Prices skyrocketed to three to four times their previous costs.

The 1980s brought electric filter coffee makers. The popularity of this batch-brew method resulted in the stagnation of the U.S. instant coffee market and the fall from grace of the dreaded percolators.

As a result of the huge coffee price increases in 1975-1976, Italian and European espresso markets substituted cheaper Robusta beans in their favorite beverage.

To this day, approximately half of Italian espresso is still made with Robusta bean filler which has a higher caffeine content. The European market has become accustomed to the cheaper Robusta based espresso which continues to represent a high percentage of consumption.

Although espresso is not considered a gourmet drink in Italy due to the use of lower quality Robusta beans, the national consumption of espresso has become part of Italian history and culture.

Italy now has over 200,000 coffee bars.

In Italy espresso is considered so essential to daily life that the price is regulated by the government.

Dr. Ernesto Illy of Italy's Illy Caffe is considered one of the world's foremost experts in coffee and espresso research. He holds a degree in chemistry. His work ranges from the study of physiological effects of coffee on the body to his current project—genetic engineering techniques applied to coffee plants.

Dr. Illy has been in charge of Illycaffe s.p.a. in Trieste, Italy, since 1963. His father, Francisco, started Illycaffe. Francisco developed the pressurization packaging of coffee to hold in the volatile oils and gasses in beans and grounds.

As late as the year 1976 people drank horrible coffee. At least 86% of the American people claimed they drank their home coffee from percolators (electric and stove-top). *Coffee,* written by Charles and Violet Schafer and published in 1976, pictures various coffeemaker types of the day, including the new filter drip cone maker. The drip cone would revolutionize traditional coffee brewing.

The new moderation evident in attitudes throughout the world in the 1980s inspired the popularity of mocktails and gourmet coffee beverages.

By the mid 1980s, upscale coffee bars featuring espresso beverages, an array of fresh roasted gourmet coffees, and coffee accessories, had appeared on the U.S. landscape.

The French philosopher, Voltaire, reportedly drank fifty cups of coffee a day.

Drinking coffee is considered to be a religious or social ritual in many countries.

In Greece and Turkey the oldest person is always served his coffee first.

In the ancient Arab world coffee became such a staple in family life that one of the causes allowed by laws for marital separation was a husband's refusal to produce coffee for his wife.

Raw coffee beans soaked in water and spices are chewed like candy in many parts of Africa.

How do you stop an asthma attack? Drink a cup of coffee … so states *The Doctor's Book of Home Remedies*.

Regular coffee drinkers have about one-third fewer asthma symptoms than noncoffee drinkers according to a Harvard researcher who studied 20,000 people.

A 1993 medical report states that drinking up to three cups of coffee a day during pregnancy is probably safe.

---

In the last three centuries 90% of all people living in the Western world have switched from tea to coffee.

---

A ten-year follow-up study of 128,000 patients in a medical research program found that the chance of suicide fell as people drank more coffee. The same study found no overall difference in the death rates between those who drank coffee and those who didn't.

---

Coffee represents 75% of all the caffeine consumed in the United States.

---

Retail espresso vendors report an increase in decaffeinated sales in the month of January due to New Year's resolutions to decrease caffeine intake.

---

Coffee consumption throughout the world is dictated by the quality of the coffee available. If only low quality coffee is available, coffee consumption is low. If high quality coffee is available, then consumption is high.

In 1993 only 11.8% of the U.S. population drank instant coffee, down 31% in the two-year period since 1991. The 1993 result is less than half the reported consumption in 1974 when the percentage of instant coffee drinkers peaked.

The British are sophisticated people in almost everything except their choice of coffee. They still drink instant ten-to-one over fresh brewed coffee.

Japan ranks number three in the world for coffee consumption.

Over 15,000 coffee cafes and several thousand vending machines dispensing both hot and cold coffee serve the needs of Tokyo alone.

In Japan coffee shops are called Kissaten.

Japanese companies have not only bought up virtually all the Jamaican Blue Mountain coffee crop, but the highest grades of many other coffee crops also. Their passion for the finest coffee and coffee related technology abounds.

For reducing wrinkles and improving their skin, the Japanese have been known to bathe in coffee grounds fermented with pineapple pulp.

Australians consume 60% more coffee than tea, a sixfold increase since 1940.

What made Sao Paulo the biggest city in South America? The coffee trade.

The world can be divided into nations of coffee drinkers and nations of tea drinkers.

Scandinavia has the world's highest per capita annual coffee consumption at 26.4 pounds. Italy has an annual coffee consumption per capita of only ten pounds.

Finland has excellent quality coffee and high coffee consumption. Conversely, there are Italy and Great Britain, with poor quality coffee and the lowest coffee consumption of the European countries.

The Brazilian plantation frosts of 1975-76 raised coffee prices worldwide and resulted in smaller price gaps between standard and gourmet coffee. Customers were willing to spend the small premium for gourmet coffee and the gourmet specialty coffee market was born.

Full-bodied coffee has become more popular in recent years, among the trends of the gourmet coffee revolution.

U.S. coffee consumption peaked in the early 1960s when 75% of the population drank more than four cups of coffee a day.

The annual U.S. per capita coffee consumption in 1991 was just over ten pounds, much less than in the 1960s or even the 1970s.

---

 The average annual coffee consumption of the American adult is 26.7 gallons, or over 400 cups.

---

 In 1990 over four billion dollars in coffee was imported into the United States.

---

 The United States consumes over one-third of the world's coffee, while Brazil produces about one-quarter to one-third of the world's coffee; each is a world leader in consumption and production.

---

 Worldwide, there are over 400 billion cups of coffee consumed each year.

---

 The 26 million acres on this globe devoted to the cultivation of coffee generate employment for over 30 million people: One of every 177 inhabitants on the planet is employed in the coffee industry. The fruit of this labor is consumed by more than one-third of the world's population.

---

 Coffee as a world commodity is second only to oil.

The modern day espresso street vending cart evolved from a Boeing Company shuttle cart purchased from surplus. The first cart was initially utilized to serve espresso at an arts and crafts fair in Edmonds, Washington, before being moved to downtown Seattle.

---

After traveling the fair circuit, the first espresso cart found a semi-permanent home under Seattle's Monorail in 1978. An explosion of self-contained espresso carts followed. By 1994 over 450 such carts operated in the Seattle area alone.

---

Popularity of espresso grew quickly, and Seattleites, enamored with the brew, have made espresso a necessity for coffee consumers.

---

Nordstrom, a Seattle-based, prestige department store chain, opened its first espresso cart in 1982 in downtown Seattle. It is estimated that each of its carts averages over 1,000 customers per day.

---

Espresso street cart vending is the biggest food and beverage marketing trend to happen in the United States since fast food drive-ins. Elsewhere, street cart vendors have marketed soft pretzels, hot dogs, ice cream, fresh produce, shrimp, cold pop, lemonade, and sassafras tea.

---

A "Coffee Community" movement is gaining momentum whereby Seattle's espresso cart licensing rules would become a national model.

When espresso carts must rent outside space from an anchor retail business, the cost usually totals 5% to 12% of total sales.

 Over a hundred different varieties of coffee are imported into the United States each year.

 Economic downturns have little effect on retail sales of espresso beverages. A cup of gourmet coffee or espresso is one of the "affordable luxuries," according to the CEO of a major U.S. coffee retailer.

## Espresso businesses generally fall into these categories:

*Espresso Cafe:* features espresso by the drink but serves at least two meals (usually breakfast and lunch).

*Espresso Bar:* features espresso and gourmet coffees by the drink and whole bean. Serves no meals, only pastries and gifts.

*Espresso Vending Carts:* sidewalk or indoor carts that feature espresso beverages, Italian sodas, and pastries.

*Drive-thru Espresso:* a small stationary building serving espresso beverages, Italian sodas, and pastries to customers in their cars through serving windows.

*Drive-up Espresso:* normally an espresso cart positioned so that customers can pull up and order in their cars.

*by Rich Abker*

The gourmet coffee industry has spawned many cottage industries: espresso carts, coffee bars, equipment purveyors and service specialists, and those who manufacture and sell the products and accessories.

 Booming gourmet retail coffee franchise opportunities for the 1990s are offered up by many U.S. and Canadian retail coffee chains. Personal investment for a franchise coffee store is minimal when compared to a franchise fee for a major fast food outlet. For an independent entrepreneur the total investment for an espresso cart completely outfitted with inventory can be less than $25,000. With equipment lease programs many successful cart operators have achieved their start-up with less than $10,000.

 Retail espresso and coffee stores are finding an ever increasing number of local cash-and-carry wholesale stores where they may purchase their syrups, supplies, and accessories.

 National wholesale distributors such as the ten-year-old RSVP International in Seattle offer espresso products, supplies, and accessories to the fast growing retail coffee market.

 Health regulations and city ordinances vary widely from state to state in governing operations of espresso vending carts.

Stateside espresso cart entrepreneurs are having great difficulty penetrating the Japanese market. The Japanese customarily take coffee sitting down and find it an awkward sensation to sip while walking.

---

A barista is said to be "slammed" when he is bombarded with business (usually five or more people waiting to be served).

---

In 1991 Japanese inventor Enomoto created a fully automatic roaster/grinder/drip brewer, all-in-one. The unit is controlled by an electronic chip and from roasting through brewing, requires 17 minutes to produce six cups of coffee.

---

One forecaster claims that by the year 2000, 50% of coffee consumed at home will be brewed in home espresso machines.

# COFFEE AND INDUSTRY TRENDS
# INTO THE YEAR 2000
## *The Shape of the Future*

1. **Espresso and Coffee Bars as the Soda Fountains of the 1950s**

   With the sale of gourmet coffee increasing almost 20% each year and the increase in the number of people abstaining from alcohol, the stage is now set for the revitalization of the 1950s soda fountain as a coffee bar.

2. **Neighborhood Sidewalk Espresso Carts throughout the U.S.**

   Espresso street cart vending is the biggest food and beverage marketing trend to happen in the United States since fast food drive-ins. The Specialty Coffee Association of America projects that by the year 1999, some 10,000 coffee cafes, espresso bars, and carts will be in operation in the U.S.

3. **Switch from Canned Coffee to Gourmet Whole Bean Coffee**

   Americans are demanding more from their coffee. In 1979 the number of U.S. supermarkets selling specialty coffee was 5,025. By 1989, it quadrupled to 20,200. The Specialty Coffee Association of America projects this number to reach 31,500 by 1999. Nationally this gourmet specialty market has reached 30% of total coffee sales by 1994.

4. **Switch to Preflavored Whole Bean Coffee**

   By 1994 flavored whole bean coffee sales represented 40% of the total specialty coffee market. This has been the fastest growing segment of the industry.

## 5. Afternoon Decaf Culture

With a multitude of coffee bars and sidewalk espresso cafes populating the landscape, Americans have adopted the German social institution of the afternoon *kaffeeklatsch*. Gone is the afternoon "happy hour." It's now the afternoon cup, sans caffeine or more commonly called a "nofun" or a "sleeper." Many restaurants seeking to fill empty seats during the afternoon dead time are finding a new profit center with decaf espresso based beverages.

## 6. Increase in Organic Coffee Consumption

Elan Imports, leading U.S. supplier of organic coffees, sold 1.5 million pounds of organic coffee in 1992. In 1993 this figure was two million pounds. By 1997 Elan projects sales of their organic coffee at ten million pounds. If coffee is to be officially classified as organic, the grower's methods must be certified. The coffee is more costly, but health-conscious consumers are starting to line up.

## 7. Italian Style Syrups
### *For flavoring sodas and espresso beverages*

In 1990 there were only a handful of manufacturers of Italian style syrups represented in the U.S. Today over 20 companies (mostly U.S. based) are promoting over 90 separate flavor varieties. Sales have skyrocketed as Italian style sodas and flavored espresso beverages reach for the $48 billion per year canned and bottled soda market.

## 8. Proliferation of Steamed Milk, Espresso Based Beverages
### *Throughout the U.S. and the world*

Ninety percent of all espresso beverages in the U.S. are served with steamed milk. With the espresso craze spreading like wildfire throughout the U.S., dairies have certainly become one beneficiary of the boom. Mochas and lattes, the two most popular of these beverages, require seven ounces of milk for each shot of espresso. One large coffee retailer in 1993 sold 2½ million gallons of milk in Washington State alone, making that coffee retailer the largest non-institutional buyer of milk in Washington State.

### 9. Use of 2% and Nonfat Milk for Espresso Based Beverages

The majority of espresso bars use 2% milk with all their standard espresso based beverages. Two percent not only foams better than whole milk, it also placates the ever diet-conscious consumer. One Northwest publication, when referring to Seattle taste preferences for lattes and mochas, called Seattle a "skinny milk" (nonfat milk) town.

### 10. Nondairy Substitutes for Milk Based Espresso Beverages

Lactase is an enzyme which allows the body to digest the milk sugar lactose. It is estimated that 70% of the world's population suffers from lactase deficiency. Asian, Mediterranean, Arab, African and Southern Italian peoples are especially prone to this deficiency. For those who love their lattes, but suffer from milk allergies, there are soybean, rice, almond, and potato milk "alternatives." All are either high in calories or sodium, and some carry a strong flavor. The proponents of the dairy-based whey alternative claim it tastes like milk and is no more expensive.

### 11. Boutique Exhibition Coffee Roasters in Your Neighborhood

In the 1970s and the 1980s, the U.S. experienced the wave of microbreweries. As the espresso and gourmet coffee wave moved in, with it came microcoffee roasters. Many of these roasters will be exhibition-style. Exhibition coffee roasters have already established themselves in such locations as upscale delis, supermarkets, gift and antique stores, and gambling casinos. All these locations feature espresso bars and, of course, showcase their roasters with the aromas as drawing cards.

### 12. U.S. Households Switch to Espresso Coffee Made at Home

With an estimated one million home espresso machines in use in the U.S. in 1994, the future market for this appliance should mushroom at least until the year 1999. One leading coffee industry expert projected that by 1999 one-half of U.S. households will make their espresso with a home espresso machine. One half represents 50 million households with new machines. If this projection materializes, retailers will sell 49 million units. As Christmas gifts home espresso machines ranked close to the top for 1992 and 1993 in dollar sales.

### 13. Gourmet Exotic Coffee Makers for Home Use

Elegant home entertaining with a social beverage that stimulates conversation: It's now made easy with a vast array of home coffee brewing devices. Visually impressive, the units brew coffee with good to excellent results. From the inexpensive, hot selling French Press (price range $20 to $50) to the very opulent and "showy" Retro® coffee maker (price range $175 to $300), exotic brewing devices increasingly appear tableside at elegant home dinner parties.

### 14. The "Americano" as a Gourmet Cup of Coffee

Two major Northwest area roaster/retailers in the April 1994 issue of *WC&T* magazine were quoted regarding this strong trend. Americans are now expecting more out of their cup of coffee. Especially for those who like their coffee straight, the gourmet "Americano" is the answer.

### 15. Bookstore Espresso Bars

A bookstore in Washington State put in an espresso bar and recorded a 46% increase in book sales. Many major book store chains in the U.S. are now packaging their new outlets with espresso bars. Some bookstores dealing in used books are exchanging used books for espresso.

### 16. High School Espresso Bars

Teenage coffee consumption is on the increase. The moderation trend of the 1980s and 1990s has opened the door for espresso based beverages and Italian sodas. Caffeine is no longer an issue: colas have comparable caffeine contents. In the Northwest high school espresso bars are being established, and the trend is moving to other U.S. regions.

### 17. Vending Machines Selling Quality Espresso with All Fresh Ingredients

Electronic, mechanical, and refrigeration technologies have been merged, resulting in consistent quality espresso beverages via the "robot" vending machine. Copy centers, office centers, and other nonfood locations are currently installing this labor-free marvel. Customers flavor their brew from a syrup rail adjacent to the machine.

### 18. Widening Espresso Marketing Avenues

As espresso bars proliferate in the U.S. landscape, the locations for these profit centers are only limited by imagination. Such is the popularity of espresso in Seattle that businesses featuring it include hardware stores, car washes, salons, department stores, nurseries, hospitals, bike shops, and even one dentist whose marquee advertises "Espresso Dental."

### 19. Espresso's Appeal to Wide Socio-economic and Ethnic Cross Sections

Originally thought of as sellers of beverages that would only have "snob" appeal, espresso businesses have not only succeeded but have prospered in blue-collar areas. Truck stops, factories, and mixed ethnic areas are now homes to busy espresso bars.

### 20. Popularity of Caffeine as a Stimulant at Work, at School, and in Social Contexts

New awareness of research studies showing caffeine's effect on increasing alertness have people flocking to this magic brew. Students at test time, long haul truckers on the road, to hospital employees are now standing in line for their espresso.

### 21. Latte Commuting

The domed snap-on traveling lid for paper cups allows spillfree commuting. These lids contain the heat and are tailor-made for espresso commuting. U.S. auto manufacturers have promoted their coffee-friendly 1994 vehicles featuring multiple built-in cup holders.

### 22. Coffee Tasting as a Social Event

Lured by more than 100 separate varieties of coffee bean and thousands of custom blends, coffee connoisseurs are increasingly testing the variations. Coffee tasting has become an event of the 1990s.

### 23. Global Espresso Proliferation

As of June 1994 the USA's largest retail gourmet coffee chain announced it would go global with an ultra dark roasted product. Other stateside entrepreneurs have branched offshore to enter new markets. The future will bring more product proliferation. Many introductions will feature nondairy substitutes designed to overcome the lactase deficiency of 70% of the world's population.

**24. Theatrical Espresso Bartenders (Baristas)**
As the espresso movement spreads, competition has forced baristas to outperform one another to increase sales. Their theatrical performances include: the sights, sounds, and aroma of grinding fresh beans; the sight and sounds of steaming milk; the portioning (dosing) and packing of ground coffee in the brew basket; the sight and aroma of extracting the espresso brew; and the mixing and garnishing of these ingredients. Some baristas add interest to their performances by adeptly juggling paper cups, syrup bottles, and like items.

**25. It Was Tea Etiquette—Now It's Espresso Etiquette.**
Proper tea etiquette dictates the order of service: first tea, then in proper order cream, sugar, cookies, and mints. In their stride, espresso-crazed Northwest-erners have developed their very own espresso slang after more than 15 years of heavy consumption. This slang, or "espresso speak," dictates order of service according to the beverage's ingredient, portions, and cup size. "Espresso speak" is moving south and east and is destined to go global.

**26. Italian Food and Dessert/Espresso Sales Tie-in**
Espresso, with its deep roots in Italian cuisine has spawned demand for food products that are indigenous to Italy. Italian desserts such as Biscotti and Tiramisu, and Italian Panini sandwiches are great tie-ins to the beverage.

## 27. Canned, Iced Espresso Based Beverages Instead of Soda Pop

Iced coffee in a can, introduced to Japan in 1945, has become the "red hot" beverage of the 1990s. With yearly sales of more than $5 billion, or 38% of all canned beverages sold in Japan, it continues to exceed the sales of colas. The iced coffee market worldwide achieved total sales of $10 billion per year by 1994. European and Pacific Rim countries account for the bulk of this business.

## 28. Granita, the Yuppie Slushies of the 1990s

One busy coffee bar owner likens the product of the granita machine to an "espresso milkshake," somewhere between a Slurpee® and a sorbet. During hot weather, espresso bars and carts sell more granitas than hot espresso beverages. Granitas, the "Italian Yuppie Slushies," come in a dazzling array of fruit flavors as well as espresso based flavors with nondairy creamers. A real growth product!

## 29. Cooking with Coffee & Italian Style Syrups

New cooking-with-coffee cookbooks are appearing almost weekly. On the shirt-tail of the coffee books are food articles and booklets featuring dessert and food recipes utilizing the full spectrum of Italian style flavored syrups. Look for expanding displays of these syrups in your neighborhood supermarkets.

## 30. Espresso Information Explosion
### *Books, videos, and retail-sponsored education outreach programs*

Many excellent books, business start-up manuals, kits, and "how to" videos on the espresso craze are now available in your locale. Coffee trade magazines are selling subscriptions. Industry associations (local and national) such as the Specialty Coffee Association of America (SCAA) are rapidly gaining members. Some retail coffee stores are providing coffee education outreach programs to community clubs and groups. The coffee information age is even moving to the information superhighway.

### 31. Eco-Espresso
The popular environmental concerns of the "new age," have inspired many take-out coffee bars to provide their own refillable coffee cups for their patrons. Unbleached paper filters and reusable filters are now being marketed for drip coffee makers.

### 32. Coffee Art, Fashion, and Accessory Items
Used burlap coffee bags made into fashion clothing such as "Java Jackets," coats, and skirts have become fashion statements of the 1990s. Coffee art, jewelry, and household accessories can be found throughout any shopping center. These coffee-culture fashion items are being merchandised in many coffee bars and have become separate profit centers for the retailer.

### 33. Higher Coffee Prices
The weekend cold snap in June 1994 destroyed approximately 25% of the next year's coffee crop in Brazil, the world's largest coffee producing country. July 1994 prices for coffee jumped to double the price of just a few months prior, the highest since November 1986. An increase of 50¢ a pound at wholesale for the world's second cheapest beverage— only water is cheaper—would still reflect only a few cents increase on the retail price of a cup of coffee.

### 34. Tea and Tea Lattes

A feature story in the July 1994 issue of *Fresh Cup* magazine stated that "Tea is the next obvious beverage trend," and that "the ready-to-drink iced tea category has tripled in revenue since 1991 to an estimated $1.2 billion in 1994." New for the 1990s are "tea lattes" with tea instead of coffee in combination with steamed milk. These delicious beverages are great when flavored with Italian style syrups. The R. Torre company, located in San Francisco (manufacturers of Torani Italian style syrups), has been influential in this movement.

### 35. High-Tech Espresso Bars of the Future

The coffee craze has attracted a well educated group of pioneering high-tech people: Innovation abounds. Technical advances in brewing equipment and techniques will be your assurance of premium quality products. The future will see a multitude of electronic wizardry such as "voice recognition" ordering, (one California company has developed mini FM stations with order transmitters for drive-up ordering). Video, audio, and lighting imagery to create moods and theme atmospheres are currently being tested.

### Other Emerging Trends into the Year 2000:

+ Office coffee service featuring gourmet coffee and espresso
+ Espresso catering
+ Retail coffee stores featuring selections from a variety of roasters
+ Separate steam frothing machines for home use
+ Coffee bars featuring fresh squeezed juices

## Fads and Trends
### *Life cycles*

✦ **Fad**    Is usually a custom that is adapted by many people with undue zeal for only a short period of time. A "passing fashion" as such, quick to catch on and quick to die.

✦ **Trend**    Has a much longer life cycle than a fad. Many trends take a few years to materialize before a long crest period, (often lasting several years) and are slow to fade.

Gerald Celente, director of the Trends Research Center in New York, states that, "Once you've identified a trend, it's important to understand where it is in its life cycle." He lists the life cycle of all trends as such: birth, growth, maturity, decline, and dying.

It is widely agreed that the most accurate method for forecasting trends is the "content analysis technique," popularized by John Naisbitt in his blockbuster 1980s publication *Megatrends*. According to Naisbitt, trends are generated from the bottom up; fads from the top down.

The content analysis technique for predicting trends consists of accumulating the amount of newsprint from daily newspaper publications (large and small), devoted to any given subject. By charting the total newsprint allocated to a subject over a period of time, weights or strengths of popularity of any subject can be assigned and its future popularity forecasted when compared vis a vis other subjects.

Relating to the coffee and beverage industry, we have utilized this "content analysis technique" for determining the hot trends into the year 2000.

# Chapter 4

# The Coffee Bean: Growing, Harvesting, Processing, Roasting

Two species of coffee beans are of economic significance.

1. ***Coffea arabica***—commonly called Arabica, grows best in altitudes beyond 3,000 feet above sea level. This species is considered a high quality bean and produces very flavorful and aromatic coffee. Arabica trees require more rigid growing requirements and are more expensive. The beans are low in caffeine, low in acidity, and high in flavor and aroma.

2. ***Coffea robusta or canephora***—commonly called Robusta, grows best in altitudes that are below 2,000 feet above sea level. Robusta is less flavorful and less aromatic than Arabica. This species is normally purchased as a "filler" bean for canned coffees in order to reduce roasters' costs. Robusta is also widely used in instant coffees. This is not the bean that is normally used by gourmet coffee roasters. It has twice the caffeine of Arabica, is high in acidity, low in flavor and aroma, and is the least expensive.

Coffee trees are evergreen and grow to heights above 15 feet. Under cultivation they are normally pruned to around eight feet in order to facilitate harvesting.

 The world's most valuable agricultural commodity is the coffee bean.

 Coffee trees produce highly aromatic, short-lived white flowers producing a scent between jasmine and orange. These blossoms produce cranberry-sized coffee cherries. Four to five years are required to yield a commercial harvest.

 Coffee cherries begin in a green stage then turn yellow, orange, red and dark crimson when ripe. Coffee cherries must be picked ripe to yield the best coffee. Each coffee cherry normally produces two green seeds that are flat on one side and concave on the other. These green seeds are the coffee beans. The green beans must have their silverskins and parchments removed before roasting.

 Only 25% of the coffee plant's flowers produce mature beans.

 Green coffee beans are nonvolatile until roasted. In fact, green beans that are stored while still maturing in their silverskins and parchments can be stored for years if cared for properly. These green beans are referred to as pergamino beans (parchment beans).

When green coffee seeds fail to divide into two seeds, they form one concave seed called a peaberry. Peaberries can be very flavorful due to their unique development and demand a high price.

Arabica constitutes 75% of the world's coffee production, but only the top 10% of Arabicas have fine enough characteristics to meet specialty coffee standards.

Arabica is the original coffee plant. It still grows wild in Ethiopia.

Coffee trees are planted in nurseries and later transplanted to the fields. When mature, they flower at the beginning of the wet season and are generally picked at the end of the dry season.

Coffee beans are similar to wine grapes in that they are affected by the temperature, soil conditions, altitude, rainfall, drainage, and degree of ripeness when picked.

A coffee plant requires more than 70 inches of water per year to thrive.

The red coffee cherries are known as drupes. Unlike such other drupes as cherries and peaches, coffee is consumed by throwing away the fruit, then roasting, grinding, brewing, and consuming the pits.

It takes about five years for an Arabica coffee plant to mature and produce its first crop (about two pounds).

The Arabica coffee bean requires only six to eight weeks after flowering before the fruit fully ripens. The Robusta bean takes nine to eleven weeks to ripen.

Coffees grown at higher elevations generally exhibit finer qualities than those grown at lower elevations.

Organic coffee is grown without the use of insecticides, herbicides, growth regulators, or synthetic fertilizers.

Coffee buyers separate the world's coffee production into three main categories: High-grown Mild Arabica, Brazilian Arabica, and Robusta.

Of the several species of coffee trees, 99% are represented by either the Arabica or Robusta types.

More than 100 kinds of coffee beans are grown commercially in 59 countries throughout the tropical regions of the world.

The first historical blend of coffee was the mocha-java, still a popular blend today.

The rarest premium coffee on earth is Jamaican Blue Mountain: Only 100,000 pounds are produced each year. The Japanese buy up practically all of this green gold.

The Japanese tend to favor a lighter roast than North Americans.

Java led the world in coffee production until rust disease almost destroyed the coffee industry there.

Between 1740 and 1805, coffee cultivation achieved its widest expansion in Central and South America.

Coffee is grown more widely in South America than on any other continent.

Brazil and Colombia together produce approximately 45% of the world's coffee.

Brazil accounts for almost one-third of the world's coffee production, producing over 3⅓ billion pounds of coffee each year.

Brazil is the largest producer and exporter of coffee, and the United States is by far the greatest consuming country in the world.

Colombia is the world's second largest coffee producer.

The Indonesian islands are the world's third largest producer of coffee. Out of over 13,000 islands, only ten produce coffee, and of those, three produce 90% of the total crop: Java, Sumatra, and Sulawesi (formerly Celebes).

---

Arabica represents only 10% of Indonesia's production, and only a fraction of this amount is considered exceptional. This small portion of select gourmet coffee is highly coveted by the select roasters.

---

Although coffee is grown around the globe, along a narrow subtropical belt, Australia with its limited production is the clear exception located outside coffee's typical geographical range.

---

Kona coffee growers, like most coffee growers, start their Arabica trees from seed in nurseries. The best trees are hand-selected for planting in the growers' field estates.

---

Hawaii is the only state of the United States in which coffee is commercially grown.

---

In 1974 "The Coffee Store" opened in Honolulu as Hawaii's first specialty coffee store.

---

Hawaii features an annual Kona Festival which includes a coffee picking contest. Each year the winner becomes a state celebrity.

In the tropical and subtropical regions where they are grown, estate coffees are confined to a specific region with the farmer specializing in only the coffee crop.

---

In Hawaii coffee is harvested between November and April.

---

Over five million people in Brazil are employed by the coffee trade. Most of those are involved with the cultivation and harvesting of more than 3 billion coffee plants.

---

The 2,000 Arabica coffee cherries it takes to make a roasted pound of coffee are normally picked by hand as they ripen. Since each cherry contains two beans, about 4,000 Arabica beans are required to make a pound bag of roasted coffee.

---

The *Gourmet Retailer* magazine states that more hand labor goes into a pound of coffee than goes into a pound of any other food product.

---

A plantation worker typically picks 150 pounds of ripe coffee cherries daily. This harvest equates to approximately 30 pounds of roasted product. A picker's daily pay is equivalent to just a few U.S. dollars.

---

After the coffee cherries are picked, they are checked for impurities, washed, processed, dried, and then graded.

The removal of the three sets of skin and their attendant layers of pulp is accomplished by pressing and hulling machines.

 After the coffee bean is picked and the outer layers of skin have been removed, it is soaked. The pulp is then fermented off the beans, which are again soaked and washed, then dried on open air patios or in drying machines.

 During a drying-out period which lasts approximately twenty days, coffee beans are raked frequently to reduce any molding.

 An alternative method for processing coffee cherries is the Dutch (WIB) method. The coffee berries are stoned to separate the beans from skin and pulp. This approach accelerates the drying process.

 Rain and high humidity are harmful to the coffee berries during the drying-out period.

 The last two crumbly layers of skin remaining on the dry bean are removed by tumbling. Once the last bits of skin have been shaken free, the beans are polished to improve their appearance.

 After harvest, coffee beans are hulled and graded by size and weight. The largest beans are usually considered premium. Although the coffee industry generally considers the large beans a good grade, size has no relation to taste or aroma.

# COFFEE BEAN
# VARIOUS STAGES

The coffee tree's white blossoms are sweet smelling, resembling orange blossoms and Jasmine. They eventually develop into small cherries, at first green, then they ripen into a bright crimson fruit.

**WHITE COFFEE BLOSSOM**

Nature has taken great care in protecting the coffee bean by surrounding it with three skins and one layer of pulp.

**UNRIPE COFFEE GREEN CHERRY**

**RIPE COFFEE RED CHERRY**

**GREEN UNROASTED COFFEE BEANS**

**BROWN ROASTED COFFEE BEANS**

Each coffee cherry normally contains two coffee beans.

# COFFEE ROASTER

Depending on variety, coffee beans are generally roasted for 10 to 20 minutes at a temperature of 400 to 500°F.

The roasted beans are unloaded into the cooling hopper and stirred mechanically while cool air is blown through them to prevent overcooking. Water is sometimes sprayed into the cooling air.

Earthy and wild flavors can be caused by careless or primitive processing of the coffee bean. Such characteristics are usually not desirable.

---

The three criteria for grading coffee are: 1) quality of the species and the altitude in which it is grown; 2) size and appearance; and 3) "cup quality"—its taste and aroma.

---

Green coffee beans fall into one of the four following categories, whose names refer to the length of time the beans have been stored: 1) new crop; 2) old crop; 3) mature crop; 4) aged or vintage beans which have been stored six to ten years under climatically controlled conditions.

---

Coffee is bought and sold as many as four or five times before it reaches the end consumer.

---

Coffee sacks are usually made of hemp and weigh approximately 132 pounds when full of green coffee beans. More than 600,000 beans are needed to fill a coffee sack.

---

Before roasting, some green coffee beans are stored for years, and experts believe that certain beans improve with age if stored properly.

---

As they age, green coffee beans lose some of their acidity and can gain body.

Coffee is picked, sorted, cleaned, bagged, roasted, and then re-bagged.

 The most important factors that influence the taste and aroma of coffee are: the type and quality of coffee beans; freshness; degree of roast; size of grind and proper extraction method; and the cleanliness of the espresso machine.

 Until the late 1800s people roasted their coffee at home. Popcorn poppers and stove-top frying pans were favored.

 The vast majority of small specialty coffee roasters in the U.S. purchase their beans from importers in San Francisco or New York City.

 Roasters strive for two important elements when creating a blend: 1) flavor quality of the beans; and 2) consistency.

 When creating an espresso blend, roasters strive for a balanced flavor—a minimal amount of bitterness, the right acidity, and the maximum amount of sweetness.

 Blending varieties of coffee for the ultimate taste requires combining those beans that complement one another, with characteristics that enhance the final product.

No coffee can simply be blended by recipe. Too many variables subtly impact taste. Commercial roasters reassemble blends often to maintain desired flavors. Maintaining consistency is part of the formula.

A quality espresso blend contains anywhere from two to ten separate Arabica bean varieties.

Blends of different beans represent the vast majority of coffee available to consumers.

In Italy most beans are blended before roasting. In the U.S. some roasters blend their beans after roasting because smaller beans would be burned if roasted with larger beans, and different beans reach their flavor peaks at different roasting times.

Roasters try to achieve coffee blends which marry a strong and pleasant aroma with an enjoyable taste.

Unripe, overripe, and diseased beans, all that when roasted would give the brew undesirable off-tastes, are detected by a scanner, and are blown away before they would be dumped in the roaster.

Most roasters use a gas flame to roast beans in a rotating air drum.

Coffee is generally roasted between 400° and 425°F. The longer it is roasted, the darker the roast. Roasting time is usually from 10 to 20 minutes.

---

Roasting changes the chemical make-up of the coffee bean. The new substances developed represent about 30% of the weight of the roasted bean.

---

Beans cooling from the roaster release about 700 chemical substances that make up the vaporizing aromas.

---

Darker roasted beans contain less acid and slightly less caffeine than lighter roasted beans. Much of the caffeine and acid substance goes up the chimney during the roasting process.

---

In the roasting process, *coffeol* gathers in pockets throughout the bean. In dark roasts this substance is forced out to the surface as the moisture is lost, giving the bean an oily appearance.

---

The roasting process causes the bean to swell and the size to increase by about 60% in volume. However, this same roasting process that inflates the bean's size also takes away between 14% and 19% of its weight.

When roasted, the coffee bean doubles in size, and the caramelization of the sugar turns it from green to brown.

There is no single shade of roast that is ideal for all coffees, but if a coffee is roasted too dark, the oils, waxes, and other flavor elements are driven to the surface and are partially dissipated in roasting.

Oily beans lose flavor quicker than those with oils still inside the bean.

The darker the roast, the more weight is lost.

When the interior of the bean reaches 400°F in the roasting process, the bean develops oils in a process called *pyolysis*, and the outer part of the bean darkens.

At the point of pyolysis, beans are dumped from the roaster and cooled immediately, normally with cold air. Misting the beans with water is an option.

Darker beans are stronger, more bittersweet, and usually have a shorter shelf life.

The burnt taste nuance produced by dark roasting effectively masks the shortcomings in flavor that a light roast will reveal. In other words, dark roasts can mask beans that are low in flavor.

Over-roasted coffee beans are very flammable during the roasting process.

 Lightly roasted coffee beans have a sharper, more acidic taste than darker roasts, which are more bittersweet.

 The traditional term "full-city" roast is used to describe a dark roast with a slight amount of oil on the surface.

 Labels given roasted coffees in the retail stores, such as Italian, French, Continental, and Viennese, do not refer to the origin of the beans. Rather they refer to the length of time the bean is roasted, a characteristic manifested by the color.

 Since the espresso boom of the early 1980s in the United States, espresso roasts have come from the more expensive Arabica bean with its lower caffeine content. Thus the myth, "only the premium espresso roasts are from Italy," can be dispelled.

 In Italy, espresso contains approximately 40% of the higher caffeinated Robusta bean.

 Arabica coffee beans contain 1-1.7% caffeine, while Robusta beans contain 2-4.5% caffeine.

In regular coffee brewing, caffeine has time to absorb into the water, resulting in 100% of the caffeine in the cup. The espresso brew method extracts only two thirds of the caffeine, while the rest is thrown away with the grounds.

A kola nut contains more caffeine than a coffee cherry.

A single shot of espresso contains 90-150 mg of caffeine. An average 8 oz cup of drip coffee contains 184 mg of caffeine.

There are about 45 milligrams of caffeine in a can of Coca-Cola©; a chocolate candy bar has about 80 milligrams of caffeine.

Studies tell us the human body will absorb only 300 milligrams of caffeine at a given time. Additional amounts are cast off and will provide no additional stimulation. The human body dissipates 20% of the caffeine in the system each hour.

MIT research indicates a 30% increase in alertness after only 30 mg of caffeine is consumed.

Milk coats the stomach lining, slowing the absorption of caffeine.

Southern Europeans roast their beans darker than northern Europeans. Southern Californians roast their beans lighter than northern Californians.

---

 In general, the West Coast favors a darker roast than the East Coast, with the Midwest somewhere in between.

Flavored coffee represents about 40% of the growing specialty coffee market.

In 1994, flavored coffees (ranked by pounds of coffee sold) were:

1 Vanilla Nut          6 Amaretto
2 Irish Cream          7 Chocolate Almond
3 Chocolate            8 Coconut
4 Vanilla              9 Cinnamon
5 Macadamia Nut   10 Chocolate Raspberry
                              Cream

Source: Flavor Technology Corporation.

In the late 1970s, the present method of flavoring coffee in its whole bean form was developed.

---

 Commercially flavored coffee beans are imbued with flavoring after they are roasted and partially cooled to around 100°F. At this temperature the coffee beans' pores are open and therefore more receptive to absorption. The flavoring agent is applied with spraying or tumbling with the beans in a kettle or a metal drum.

The April 1994 issue of *World Coffee & Tea* lists the sales breakdown of the U.S. **Gourmet Coffee Market** as:

40%   Flavored—both Regular and Decaf
25%   Selects and Blends
18%   Decaffeinated
17%   Dark Roast

Decaffeinated coffee is less popular in the Pacific Rim countries than it is in the U.S.

 In the early 1980s, only a handful of flavor varieties were available for whole bean coffee. By 1994 close to 200 separate whole bean flavors were being marketed.

 *"Flavored gourmet coffee initially served as a vehicle for introducing non-coffee drinkers to good coffee. It was an entry-level beverage in the beginning, but it has carved out its own niche now. Many people enjoy it for its own sake. It's like a dessert treat without the calories and without the fat."* The preceding quote in the April, 1994 issue of *Tea & Coffee Trade Journal* was from Michael S. Abrams, vice president of sales and marketing (flavors and fragrances) for Melchers & Co., a San Francisco-based flavor producer.

 The process by which coffee becomes decaffeinated was discovered in 1906.

 In 1993, 15% of all coffee consumed in the U.S. was decaf, down from 24% decaf consumption in 1987.

 The three major methods of decaffeinating coffee are: 1) Swiss Water Process; 2) Natural Process—Ethyl Acetate; and 3) Natural Process—Coffee Oil Process. Other less used methods are the carbon dioxide ($CO_2$) super-critical process, and the methlene chloride method.

The 40-year-old Swiss Water Process, an all-water method of decaffeinating coffee, is the trade name of Coffex, the Swiss company that patented this process. In 1988 this company moved from Switzerland to Vancouver, British Columbia, where all U.S. Swiss Water Process "decaf" coffees are treated.

The demand for Swiss Water decaffeinated coffee has increased by 64% from 1989 to 1992.

After the decaffeinating process, processing companies no longer throw the caffeine away; they sell it to pharmaceutical companies.

When roasted coffee beans are exposed to air, they begin to release carbon dioxide which carries with it the beans' vaporizing aromas.

Roasted coffee is a highly perishable product, vulnerable to moisture, light, and above all, oxygen. Oxygen can cause the coffee oil to become stale, decreasing the coffee's aroma and flavor.

Roasted coffee beans start to lose small amounts of flavor within two weeks. Ground coffee begins to lose its flavor in minutes. Brewed coffee and espresso begin to lose flavor within minutes.

A high percentage of the coffee in the United States is probably purchased stale due to improper handling and packaging.

There is no packaging technique that can remove all the air from the can. What air remains reacts with the aroma and flavor factors of ground coffee, although at a reduced rate.

---

Roasted coffee beans properly stored in an airtight container will stay reasonably fresh for only up to ten days.

---

With rare exceptions, coffee cans do not have vapor locks. After coffee is roasted it gives off carbon dioxide and cannot be vacuum-packed for several days. Otherwise the cans will explode. Perfect freshness will be lost. A vapor lock can be an important factor in reducing such losses.

---

Small one-way valves used in most of today's specialty packaging are known as "belly button valves." They allow carbon dioxide to escape the bag, relieving built-up pressure and thereby preserving freshness and adding to the shelf life of the roasted espresso beans. The valves were introduced in 1968.

---

Never freeze dark roasted espresso blends. The delicate oils on the surface of the beans jell, and the flavor is jeopardized.

---

It's best not to refrigerate your roasted coffee beans. Even if they are stored in airtight containers, the beans are very porous and will absorb even mild odors from the refrigerator.

A Tupperware® container or an airtight glass is best for the storage of coffee beans. Earl W. Tupper started Tupperware® in 1945, the same year the word *Espresso* first appeared in American print.

Store the airtight container in a slightly cool, dark place at a temperature between 50°-70°F.

Grinding accelerates the staling process by exposing more surface area of the bean to air, the number one staling agent. Each shot of espresso should be ground just prior to brewing for peak freshness.

Stale coffee becomes softer with age and therefore grinds differently from fresh coffee.

The freshness of brewed coffee normally expires after 20 minutes when the liquid has been heated in a pot on a warmer. Freshness can be preserved for up to two hours in a vacuum air pot or thermos bottle.

Marvin I. Haas, a coffee company CEO, said in the November, 1993 issue of *World Coffee & Tea*, "The sale of premium coffees and European-style espresso-based drinks for on-premise consumption is the fastest growing area in the specialty coffee business."

# ESPRESSO ACCESSORIES

Dump box for espresso grounds

Stainless steel foaming and steaming pitchers

Double shot porta-filter

Single shot porta-filter

Triple shot porta-filter with three spouts, and a brew basket that holds three eight-gram portions of ground espresso beans

Flat-based espresso hand packer

Shot glass to portion flavored syrups

Three to five ounce stainless steel creamer to collect brewed espresso. (Ceramic pouring glasses are preferred by many baristas.)

# Chapter 5

# The Barista's Supplies

Some of the many barista tools used are: milk steaming pitchers, pouring glasses, grounds box, thermometer, spoons, spatulas, cleaning and scrubbing brushes, measuring shot glass, bar towels, and hand tamper.

 The first coffee drinkers, the Arabs, flavored their coffee with spices during the brewing process.

 Sugar first replaced honey as a sweetener in European kitchens in medieval times, although it was used in China and India more than 2,000 years ago.

 The explosion of espresso based beverages across North America has generated the demand for quality flavored "Italian Style" syrups.

# Flavors of the 1990s
## Italian Style Syrup Selections

| | | |
|---|---|---|
| Almond | Cranberry | Orange |
| Amaretto | Creme de Cacao | Orange Brandy |
| Anisette | Creme de Cassis | Orange Mocha |
| Apple | Creme de Menthe | Passion Fruit |
| Apricot | Curaço Orange | Peach |
| B-52 | Egg Nog | Pear |
| Banana | French Vanilla | Pecan |
| Bavarian Bing Cherry | German Chocolate | Peppermint |
| Black Cherry | Ginger | Peppermint |
| Black Forest | Grape | Schnapps |
| Blackberry | Grapefruit | Pina Colada |
| Blue Curaçao | Green Banana | Pink Grapefruit |
| Blueberry | Grenadine | Pistachio |
| Boysenberry | Hazelnut | Praline |
| Butter Rum | Highlander Grog | Raspberry |
| Butterscotch | Irish Cream | Root Beer |
| Butterscotch Toffee | Jasmine | Rose |
| Caliente Orange | Kahlua Coffee | Rum |
| Canadian Cream | Kiwi | Sambuca |
| Caramel | Lemon | Simple Syrup |
| Cherry | Licorice | Spanish Coffee |
| Chocolate | Lime | Strawberry |
| Chocolate Fudge | Macadamia Nut | Swiss Chocolate |
| Chocolate Malt | Mandarino | Almond |
| Chocolate Mint | Mango | Tamarindo |
| Chocolate Peanut | Maple Nut | Toasted Walnut |
| Butter | Maraschino | Triple Sec |
| Chocolate Raspberry | Melon | Tropical Fruit |
| Cinnamon | Mint | Vanilla |
| Coconut | Mocha | Vanilla Nut |
| Coffee | Monte Cristo | Watermelon |
| Cola | | Wild Cherry |

# Exotic Syrups—Flavor Descriptions

| | |
|---|---|
| **Amaretto** | Comes from apricot pits and herbs; yields a pleasant almond flavor. |
| **Anisette** | An anise-based syrup, very sweet, similar to licorice. |
| **B-52** | A combination of Kahlua, Irish Cream, and Grand Marnier. |
| **Blue Curaçao** | Flavored with green peels of under-ripe oranges; pronounced CURE-A-SOW. |
| **Creme de Cacao** | Rich blend of cocoa and vanilla beans. |
| **Creme de Cassis** | Black currant flavored syrup. |
| **Creme de Menthe** | A peppermint-flavored syrup. |
| **Grenadine** | A pomegranate-flavored syrup. |
| **Irish Cream** | A slightly tangy coconut-vanilla cream-flavored syrup. |
| **Kahlua** | A Mexican coffee flavor. |
| **Kiwi** | An egg-sized fruit of subtropical origin possessing a sweet, green pulp having a strawberry-like flavor. |
| **Mandarino** | Has a tangerine flavor derived from peels of Mandarin oranges. |
| **Mango** | Similar to apricot taste, from a yellowish-red tropical fruit. |
| **Maraschino** | Derived from Dalmation Marasca cherries and their pits. |
| **Orgeat** | An almond-flavored syrup, pronounced OR-zhat. |
| **Passion Fruit** | A pleasant sweet tasting syrup from a pale-yellow small tropical fruit. |
| **Praline** | A syrup made from nut kernels boiled in sugar, with a slight hint of vanilla. |
| **Sambuca** | Flavored with anise and the witch elderberry bush, a licorice taste. |
| **Tamarindo** | A date-flavored syrup. |

## Thick Syrups

These syrups work well when decorating or garnishing with the pinched paper cup technique.

| | |
|---|---|
| Butterscotch | Marshmallow |
| Caramel | Molasses |
| Chocolate | Peanut Butter |
| Honey | |

## Miscellaneous Powders, Spices and Garnishes

| | |
|---|---|
| Allspice | Malt Powder |
| Brown Sugar | Mexican Chocolate Mix |
| Cardamom | Mixed Sprinkles |
| Chocolate, Ground Sweet | Nutmeg |
| Chocolate Sprinkles | Postem® |
| Cinnamon | Powdered Malt Cinnamon |
| Sticks | Tang™ |
| Cloves | Vanilla Powder |

# INVENTORY CHECKOFF

## Milk & Milk Products
Nonfat (Skim Milk)
2% Milk
Whole Milk
Half-and-Half
Whipped Cream
Condensed Milk
Egg Nog
Soy Milk
Milk Substitute
Butter

## Coffee
Espresso blend
Espresso decaf

## Soft Drinks
Cola
Ginger Ale
Seltzers
Seven-Up
Soda water

## Juices
Apple Juice
Grapefruit Juice
Orange Juice

Before the turn of the century the word *java* did not mean coffee. It meant "nutmeg." In native Malay, *java* translated literally as "land of nutmeg."

The first coffee drinkers in the Middle East used cinnamon to flavor their coffee.

Centuries ago on the Arabian peninsula coffee was commonly mixed with butter, molasses, and cardamom.

Citrus has been added to coffee for several hundred years.

The Europeans first added chocolate to their coffee in the 1600s.

Frederick the Great had his coffee made with champagne and a bit of mustard.

English scientist Joseph Priestley, discoverer of oxygen, invented carbonated soda water in 1767. By 1807 fruit flavors were added to the bubbly producing Nephite Julep—the world's first soda pop.

Dr. Pepper®, first sold in America in 1885, is the oldest commercial soft drink on the U.S. market.

# GARNISHES

Large colorful straws

Flavored whipped cream

Maraschino cherry

Top whipped cream with decorative swizzle

Cinnamon sticks for flavoring and stirring hot mixes

Shredded coconut

Nut slivers

Powdered spices— sweet chocolate, nutmeg, cinnamon or vanilla

Candy cane for Christmas beverages

Thick flavored syrup poured from pinched paper cup

Flavored syrups

Cookie or brownie crumbs over whipped cream

Lemon twist for iced beverages

Flavored ice cubes

Frozen grapes or berries used for ice cubes

# ITALIAN STYLE FLAVORED SYRUPS

With over 40 primary flavors now available, over 800 separate two-flavor combinations can be created.

## PREPARING*

Easy rule for hot, flavored espresso beverages:

1. Pour the flavoring first.
2. Pour the espresso second.
3. Pour the milk last.

*Heat intensifies the sweetness of sugar. Thus ½ to ¾ ounce of Italian flavored syrup is recommended to sweeten and flavor a 12 ounce hot espresso based beverage. For a 16 ounce cold beverage, filled ⅔ full with ice, a 2 ounce portion of syrup combined with soda water would be the recommended portion.

*Flavored coffee lends its popularity to the fact that just about all flavors mix well with it when used proportionally.

In 1886 an Atlanta druggist made a great discovery. When he mixed the extract of the African kola nut with the coca extract (a derivative of coca leaves) Coca-Cola® was born.

 In 1888 Marvin Stone patented the first wax-coated straw. Before that, hollow stalks of rye were used for sipping flavored beverages. Such straws often cracked.

 The ice machine was invented in 1865 and first appeared in a restaurant in New Orleans in 1875. The technology was slow to reach soda fountains and bars, however, and ice cubes weren't much in evidence until after WW II.

 The first drugstore soda fountain appeared in 1825. By 1891 fountains had become so popular that in New York City they outnumbered the saloons.

 By the 1880s, such was the popularity of the ice cream sodas that many towns in the Midwest prohibited their sales on the Christian Sabbath. By removing the carbonated water from these creations, soda fountain owners found a way of pleasing their customers without breaking the law. The Sunday soda became the Sundae.

 Iced Italian style beverages are visually appealing and should be served in clear glasses or clear plastic glasses.

Confused about the difference between soda water and seltzer? Both are carbonated. They both add sparkle to Italian sodas. Soda water or club soda is man-made and contains various sodiums and salts. Seltzer can be man-made, but is often a naturally carbonated mineral water. Seltzer contains no sodium or salt.

Soda water and seltzer are calorie free. However a typical 8 ounce serving of soda water will contain 70 mg of sodium.

*Seltzer* is derived from the German city of Nieder Selters. The term denoted a popular sparkling water consumed years ago in that city.

Italian syrups for flavoring espresso and soda beverages have been available in Europe for many years, but their actual popularity in the U.S. is fairly recent.

Aside from espresso and soda-water beverages, Italian flavored syrups are merchandised for ice cream toppings, milk shake flavorings, and desserts.

In 1874 at an exhibition in Philadelphia, Robert Green invented the ice cream soda. He ran out of cream to mix with syrup and carbonated water: Ice cream was substituted and ....

Some Italian style syrups claim to be natural or naturally flavored.

Citric and malic acids are often used as additives in Italian style syrups. They are used as stabilizers and flavor enhancers. Careful—when the acid content is too high, the syrup will curdle when blended with milk if the mixture is too hot.

Italians usually add sugar to their espresso.

Iced coffee in a can, introduced to Japan in 1945, has become the "red hot" beverage of the 1990s. With yearly sales of more than $5 billion, or 38% of all canned beverages sold, it continues to exceed the sales of colas.

The iced coffee market worldwide achieved total sales of $10 billion per year by 1994. The European and Pacific Rim countries account for the bulk of this business.

Basically, flavored syrups are made from such sugar products as fructose or a corn sweetener, water, flavoring (natural or artificial), colorings, and in some cases a stabilizer and/or a preservative.

Certain Italian style flavored syrups are especially suited for hot drinks, while others are better suited for iced Italian sodas. Generally the fruit flavors work better for the iced sodas. For hot espresso based beverages the following flavor groupings are more popular: chocolate, caramel, coffee, mints, cinnamon, vanilla, and the nut-based flavors.

Iced coffees and Italian sodas are now rivaling iced teas and soda pop as favored hot weather beverages.

---

Flavor chemists say the overwhelming use of artificial flavors has resulted in the public's preference for them over natural flavors.

---

A maraschino cherry is a cherry that has simply been dyed.

---

Among the various natural fruit juices, orange is the flavor choice of 65% of people in the United States.

---

Here's a creative way to sweeten your coffee: try individually wrapped swizzle sticks made from crystallized sugar. Stir, and they dissolve. Chocolate spoons that dissolve are another option.

---

Rhode Islanders and *only* Rhode Islanders drink a whole lot of milk mixed with coffee syrup.

---

Flavored syrup preferences vary from city to city and region to region. In Seattle, caramel and chocolate are preferred; in Portland, vanilla. Californians favor the taste of berries, and Easterners choose almond, amaretto, and coffee flavors.

Carob or other natural chocolates can be substituted for the artificial product in mochas.

Just 30 years ago a flightless New Zealand bird gave its name to a fuzzy fruit known as the Chinese gooseberry. This Kiwi soon succeeded in the export market and has subsequently become a popular flavored syrup for Italian style sodas.

Gail Borden invented condensed milk in 1856. Evaporated milk was invented in 1884 by John Meyenberg.

Of all the additives used over the centuries to enhance coffee's flavor, from sugar and honey to spirits and spices, hot frothy steamed milk has become its most popular condiment.

Some brands of milk have a shelf life of nine months and don't require refrigeration. They're made by using an ultra-high temperature to kill disease-causing bacteria. Nutritional elements are unaffected. These brands can be used for steaming lattes.

To make powdered milk, the dairies simply remove the cream from whole milk and use heat to extract water. Only dry powder remains.

Lactase is an enzyme which allows our bodies to digest the milk sugar lactose. An estimated 70% of the world's population suffers from lactase deficiency. Asian, Mediterranean, Arab and southern Italian peoples are especially prone to this deficiency.

Intolerance to milk in these regions has caused cappuccinos to be smaller or to be made with nondairy substitutes. Such substitutes are especially popular in Asia.

For those who love lattes but suffer from milk allergies, there are soybean, rice, almond, and potato milk "alternatives." They are all either high in calories or sodium and some carry a strong flavor. The proponents of the dairy-based whey "alternative" claim it tastes like milk and is no more expensive.

The whey-based product, low in calories, and with no cholesterol, is also now being offered as a milk alternative for espresso based beverages.

The dairies have certainly become beneficiaries of the espresso boom. One large retail coffee chain sold over 2½ million gallons of milk in 1993 in Washington State alone. A 12 ounce single latte requires 7 ounces of milk to a single shot of espresso.

The first Holstein cow arrived in the U.S. in 1851. Today an espresso bar selling 200 tall lattes per day will keep two of these cows working full time.

The USDA provides the following nutritional data for an 8 ounce (1 cup) serving of milk for each of the four milk varieties.

| Variety | Fat Grams | Calories | % Calories from Fat |
|---|---|---|---|
| Whole milk | 7.7 | 150 | 46 |
| 2% milk | 4.9 | 121 | 37 |
| 1% milk | 2.4 | 102 | 22 |
| Nonfat milk | 0 | 86 | 0 |

 In the Caribbean, coconuts are more common than cows. The morning coffee is often taken with coconut milk instead of the dairy product.

 An experienced practitioner recommends the following nondairy substitute for best tasting and steaming characteristics: one-third light soy milk to two-thirds rice milk. The soy milk has sufficient protein for foaming and texture, and the rice milk provides the flavor.

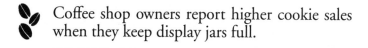 Coffee shop owners report higher cookie sales when they keep display jars full.

 Preheating the ceramic espresso cups will help to slow the coffee's flavor loss.

 Tip on foaming/steaming eggnog: mix one third 2% milk with two-thirds eggnog for better results.

Lavazza is Italy's largest coffee retailer, serving three-quarters of Italian households. The company introduced its products to American markets in the late 1980s.

Maxim®, the first freeze-dried coffee, was introduced in 1965. Two years later, Taster's Choice® (Nestlé) appeared on store shelves.

At its Turin plant, Lavazza produces about 300 tons of coffee per day. Panels of consumers periodically check the roasted and packaged coffee to insure the product's consistency.

The dried and ground root of the chicory plant is often used as an additive or substitute for coffee in Creole brewing.

During the Civil War food and coffee were scarce in New Orleans, and bitter chicory root was widely substituted for coffee. The brew's bitterness was often moderated with milk. Chicory/coffee blends continue to enjoy regional popularity.

Bibicafe®, the first pre-packaged iced coffee sold in the United States since 1985, was originally made and marketed in Italy in 1941.

Scientists tell us a beverage's thirst-quench-quotient depends on high water content. Coffee ranks fourth behind plain water (first), club soda (second), and iced tea (third). Other beverages in descending order are: diet cola, presweetened Kool-Aid®, beer, ginger ale, and milk.

---

Tiramisu (tear-a-MEE-su), one of the latest Italian dessert rages, is basically layers of ladyfingers soaked with espresso and sandwiched with fluffy clouds of eggs and Mascarpone cheese. The assembly is topped with shaved chocolate or cocoa powder.

---

Biscotti (bee-SKOAT-tee), a traditional Italian cookie, has become popular at espresso bars. Often flavored with almond and poppy seeds, biscotti are twice baked. The cookie's crunchy texture is specifically designed to be dipped.

---

Proper tea etiquette dictates first tea, then in order: cream, sugar, cookies, and mints. Such a formal service order has not yet been established for coffee. However, a popular ordering procedure for espresso based beverages has emerged and appears on the following page.

# Order Etiquette
## For Espresso Based Beverages

***Example:***
A mocha with two shots of espresso, nonfat milk, and no whipped cream, in a 12 ounce cup.

### Double Tall Skinny Whipless Mocha

| | |
|---|---|
| *Double* | Number of shots of espresso (2) |
| *Tall* | 12 ounce cup |
| *Skinny* | Milk type (nonfat) |
| *Whipless* | No whipped cream |
| *Mocha* | Name of beverage (mocha) |

Order Procedure:

1. Number shots of espresso *if* more than one.

2. Size of cup *if* other than a regular 8 ounce cup.

3. Type of milk *if* other than 2%.

4. If foam is to be withheld, state "foamless."

5. If whipping cream is to be withheld, state "whipless."

6. If beverage is to be other than latte, state name of beverage (i.e. mocha).

# Espresso Slang

| | |
|---|---|
| "A" | Americano |
| Brevé | Latte with half-and-half substituted for milk |
| Double | Two shots of espresso |
| Dry | More foamed milk—less steamed milk. (i.e. dry cappuccino). |
| Foamless | No foam |
| Grandé | 16 ounce cup |
| Harmless | Made with decaf espresso |
| Lungo | (Long pour) 1½ ounces water through a single measure of espresso |
| Nofun | Made with decaf espresso. |
| Quad | Four shots of espresso. |
| Ristretto | (Short pour) ¾-1 ounces water through a single measure of espresso. |
| Short | 8 ounce cup |
| Single | One shot of espresso |
| Skinny | Made with nonfat milk |
| Sleeper | Made with decaf espresso |
| Solo | Single shot of espresso |
| Tall | 12 ounce cup |
| Triple | Three shots of espresso. |
| Wet | More steamed milk—less foamed milk (i.e. wet cappuccino). |
| Whipless | No whipping cream. |
| With Room | Cup not completely filled with coffee, so there is room for cream. |

# COMMERCIAL ESPRESSO MACHINES

Manually operated by lever action

On/off button control; continuous pour until off is pushed

**PISTON TYPE OR MANUAL STYLE ESPRESSO MACHINE**

**SEMI AUTOMATIC ESPRESSO MACHINE**

Push button with water dosage control and automatic shut-off

Push button and computerized to serve complete drinks such as lattes and cappuccinos

**AUTOMATIC ESPRESSO MACHINE**

**FULLY AUTOMATIC ESPRESSO MACHINE**

# Chapter 6

# The Equipment

The first roasted coffee beans were boiled whole in water. Later, man ground the roasted beans with a mortar and pestle, then boiled them, which added flavor and aroma.

In 1908 Melitta Bentz, a housewife from Dresden, Germany, took blotting paper from her son's notebook and used it as a coffee filter, thus creating the world's first drip coffeemaker.

Today, nearly three-quarters of the U.S. ground roast coffee drinkers enjoy the drip method invented by this entrepreneurial woman. Succeeding generations of the Bentz family have continued the company and tradition of its founder.

The infusion method makes coffee with boiling water poured over ground coffee, the method used to make tea.

In the percolation method of brewing coffee the boiling water passes through coffee grounds by only the force of gravity.

In 1935 Italian Francisco Illy substituted compressed air for steam and produced the first automatic espresso machine.

---

In 1947 Achilles Gaggia introduced a hand lever mechanical piston to replace steam pressure. His refinement produced a fast, high pressure extraction, characterized by a thick layer of foam or crema, the signature of good espresso. Gaggia's piston could produce 130 pounds per square inch of pressure.

---

Gaggia's new method of high pressure extraction is hailed by many as perhaps the greatest development of all time in coffee brewing.

---

Crema, the heart and soul of espresso, was now achievable with Gaggia's new machine. This light-colored foam covering each shot was baffling to the Italian "experts" as Gaggia attempted to market his invention. Most prospective customers declined. By 1950 a total of only 30 of his machines were sold.

---

Prior to the emergence of the pump drive machine in 1947, steam-pressure machines could only exert 22 pounds per square inch of pressure to extract the espresso. This amount was not nearly enough pressure to produce "crema."

---

The manual or lever espresso machine was sold widely in Italy during the 1950s. This type of machine drives a piston which compresses the water into the ground beans.

In 1961 Ernesto Valente replaced the spring of the lever machine with a rotating pump driven by a small electric motor.

---

Since the pump would not work with hot water, Valente decided to compress the water while it was still cold, before it passed into the heat exchanger in the boiler of his machine. Previously the water had been first heated and then compressed.

---

In 1961 the first model of the "continuous delivery" machines was created in Italy. This is the most common machine in commercial use today.

---

The first automatic espresso machine that portioned the amount of water for a preset shot of espresso appeared in 1965.

---

The espresso machine provides energy to the water which passes through the pressed coffee grounds capturing only the best flavor essences. The two sources of this energy are pressure and heat.

---

Domestic (household) espresso machines added rotative and later vibrating pumps by the 1960s. Pressurized extraction could finally be accomplished without the cumbersome manual lever. These household units were capable of frothing the milk as well.

An Italian, Sr. Paoletti, invented a spring-loaded brew basket (porta-filter) in 1984. This basket compressed the ground coffee when the basket was twisted into the espresso machine's brew chamber. The spring-loaded device insured separation of the crema by automatically packing the grounds correctly. This type of porta-filter is a very popular feature of high-end home espresso makers.

Pre-infusion is a feature option available on a few commercial espresso machines. The brew basket is wet with hot water prior to the brew pressure being applied. This option provides the optimum extraction.

There are over 80 separate home and commercial espresso machine brands. The vast majority of these machines are manufactured in Italy.

The world's largest espresso station is owned by Chateau Miel in California, makers of ICE CAP® frosty cappuccino. The station measures 14 feet high by 12 feet long.

The United States imported only 2,000-2,500 commercial espresso machines in 1989. The number of commercial espresso machines imported in 1993 was 10,000; for 1994, 15,000.

Commercial espresso machines can be powered by one of two types of pumps: 1) compact vibrator pump; or 2) heavy duty rotary pump. Either can create 130 PSI, the optimum pressure for extracting perfect espresso.

Hard water over a period of time will cause a limescale build-up inside any espresso machine's boiler, thereby reducing its efficiency.

 The boilers of commercial espresso machines are rated by liter size. The more liter capacity, the more hot water capacity. Some manufacturers with smaller boilers increase the heating element size, thereby increasing the wattage. This increased wattage provides increased steam recovery. A wattage-to-liter-size ratio is used in determining continued steaming capacity for a better extraction.

 It can be argued that a larger boiler, providing more hot water capacity, would be useful when a high portion of Americanos are served. But in the U.S. only about 3% of the total drinks are Americanos. The vast majority of espresso beverages require steamed milk; thus the wattage-to-liter-size ratio is critical when rating a commercial machine.

 Coffee bean grinders come in two styles:
1) The more expensive burr grinder.
2) The blade grinder, similar to a miniature electric blender.

 Burr grinders are greatly preferred, as the rough metal plates flake the beans apart and don't heat and burn the bean granules as blade grinders often do. Also, blade grinders have no grind settings and must be regulated manually.

The burr grinder's wheels turn slowly, keeping the heat to a minimum, flaking the coffee beans, and exposing maximum surface area for extracting the flavor oils.

---

Much flavor is destroyed by blade grinders through heat from the violent pounding. Such grinders offer you no precise way to adjust the fineness of grind.

---

The electric blade grinder was introduced in the 1950s. It has only recently become popular in U.S. households.

---

Although the vast majority of commercial espresso machines are manufactured in Italy, a handful of brands are manufactured in the United States.

---

The Caffé Acorto, a completely automated commercial espresso machine, can make a latte in 32 seconds. The average two-group automatic espresso machine can make four lattes in slightly more time.

---

Ian Bersten's majestic tome, *Coffee Floats—Tea Sinks* (1993), states that, "The commercial espresso machine of the first half of the twentieth century was the greatest and most exciting development in the history of coffee."

# ESPRESSO CONCEPTS

Espresso is extracted by hot water under pressure, that is forced through a bed of finely ground coffee.

Early espresso machine concept after pump and heating element were added

# HOME TYPE PUMP BOILER SYSTEM ESPRESSO MACHINE

PUMP

STEAM

WATER

STEAM NOZZLE

WATER RESERVOIR

HEATING ELEMENT

PORTA-FILTER

# THE FOUR TYPES OF
# HOME MACHINES

## 1. Stove Top (Moka Maker)

Price Range—$20 up

- a. ***Does not make true espresso with crema.***
- b. Water heated to boiling in bottom of three chambers is forced up through the middle chamber containing coarse ground coffee (reverse drip), and is deposited in the top chamber.
- c. No milk steaming capability.
- d. Scalded coffee—boiling water at 212°F scalds the coffee. Correct water temperature for quality espresso is 195°F.
- e. Easy to use.

 More than 20 million Moka Makers have been sold, most in Europe since WWII.

## 2. Electric Steam Machines (Non Pump Boiler)

Price Range—$60 to $130

    a. ***Does not make true espresso with crema.***

    b. Heating element in boiler, heats water close to boiling, forcing low pressure extraction through brew chamber.

    c. Batch brewed, low pressure extraction, one to four cups at a time.

    d. Steaming attachment is tricky to use. Very poor steam capability.

    e. Caution—machine must be cooled down before removing pressure cap to refill the boiler.

## 3. Electric Piston Lever (Manual)

Price Range—$350 to $1,000

a. ***Makes excellent true espresso with crema.***

b. Exotic antique appearance.

c. A hand lever attached to a piston forces water heated by an electric element in boiler through finely ground coffee.

d. Good milk steaming capability.

e. Temperature gauge for thermostatic control over both brewing (195°F) and steaming temperature (260°F).

f. Takes practice to master manual (leverized) control of extraction.

g. Water whistling like a tea kettle during warm-up can be annoying.

# 4. Electric Pump—Pump Boiler/Pump Thermal Block

Price Range $175—$550 and up

   a. ***Better machines make excellent espresso with crema and foamed/steamed milk beverages.***

   b. These machines represent **90%** of total home machine sales.

   c. **Pump Boiler**—Most similar to commercial machines, in that water is pumped from water source (reservoir) into boiler heated by electric element. High pressure espresso extraction (aided by pump). Two separate thermostats control both extraction temperature (195°F) and the steaming temperature (260°F). Warm-up takes up to ten minutes.

   d. **Pump Thermal Block Machine**—Water is pumped through radiator type heating coils and is instantly heated to correct brewing temperature, which is controlled by one of two thermostats. Mid to high pressure extraction dependent upon pump and machine type. Separate steaming temperature thermostat. Warm-up as fast as 30 seconds.

   e. Better machines have both high pressure espresso extraction and high volume steam pressure.

# ELECTRIC PUMP ESPRESSO MACHINES
## *What to look for when purchasing a home machine:*

☐ Heavy duty over-all construction and weight of machine.

☐ Wattage of 750 or more.

☐ Two thermostats for separate control over:
   - Brewing temperature 195°F
   - Steaming temperature 260°F

☐ Extraction pressure of 6-9 atmospheres (90-130 P.S.I.); 130 P.S.I. is the optimum.

☐ Enough steam volume to foam/steam 6 oz of cold milk to a temperature of 130°F within 1½ minutes. Ask your salesperson.

☐ Does the steam wand swivel? Can a ½ liter steaming pitcher be placed under the tip of the steam wand with ease?

☐ Is porta-filter of commercial size—7 gram (Single) 14 gram (Double)—and is it of heavy duty commercial weight?

☐ Does it come with user-friendly instruction manual, a 1-800 customer assistance number, or a "how to video"?

☐ How knowledgeable is the salesperson in demonstrating the machine and answering questions?

☐ Warranty and local service considerations.

Other considerations:

Price? Size of water reservoir? Does the pump require priming before each use? Does porta-filter handle adjust for variation in the coffee grind? Capacity of drip tray, and its ease of use? Are there status indicator lights for: (1) Power; (2) When the water has reached brewing temperature; and (3) When steam has reached steam temperature?

# FOAMING ATTACHMENTS FOR HOME ESPRESSO MACHINES

The foaming attchments actually inject additional air into the milk, thus speeding the foaming process.

Beware—many lower priced home espresso machines lack the steam pressure to heat the milk adequately. A foaming attachment on one of these machines will only assist in foaming (stretching) the milk without heating it to the recommended temperature of 140°F.

# GRINDERS

Burr assembly

The top burr is stationary while the bottom burr rotates.

The closer the burrs are to each other, the finer the grind.

Blades

Commercial electric
burr grinder and doser

Home-type electric
blade grinder

# THE TWO TYPES OF HOME COFFEE GRINDERS

The exact fineness of the grind is much more critical with espresso than with drip coffee.

## 1. Electric Blade Grinders

Price Range—$15 to $30

    a.   The electric blade grinder introduced in the 1950s has only recently become popular in U.S. households. It is similar to a miniature electric blender.

    b.   Blade grinders destroy much of the coffee's flavor through heat from the violent pounding.

    c.   Inexpensive blade grinders are quick and can be used for flavored coffees.

    d.   These units have no grind settings for the precise, uniform grind necessary for quality espresso. Just *On* and *Off.*

---

**Appropriate Time for Grinding Coffee Beans with Electric Blade Grinder:**

| | |
|---|---|
| Drip Grind | 20-30 seconds |
| Espresso Grind | 40-50 seconds |

---

# 2. Burr-Wheel Grinders

Price Range—$150 to $400 Home Type
$500 to $1,000 Commercial Type

a. The burr grinder's wheels turn slowly, keeping the heat to a minimum, flaking the coffee beans, and exposing maximum surface area for extracting the flavor oils.

b. Be warned that flavored coffees may flavor the coffee grinder burrs, which can in turn flavor high quality coffee beans ground later. It is nearly impossible to clean the burr-wheels completely.

c. Most units have an adjustable dosing mechanism that measures the amount of ground coffee dispensed into the porta-filter (brew basket).

d. Burr grinders are greatly preferred because the rough metal plates flake the beans apart and don't heat and burn the bean granules as blade grinders often do.

e. The grind settings are tricky and must be constantly fine tuned to compensate for the many variables: humidity, degree of roast, and the bean density.

f. A burr-wheel grinder-doser is required for the optimum espresso grind.

*Antique
Burr-wheel
Grinder*

# ESPRESSO MACHINE COMPARISON

| Home Machines | Commercial Machines |
|---|---|
| Must refill water manually. Waste water drains into drip tray that must be emptied. | Plumbed into an in-line water supply and a direct drain. |
| Unable to extract espresso and foam/steam milk simultaneously. **Two separate operations are required** because espresso is extracted at 195°F and milk is foamed/steamed at 260°F. After the espresso extraction (195°F), the heating element inside the boiler must switch to a high-heat setting. A typical waiting period of **30 seconds** is required before the boiler is super-heated to 260°F and steaming can proceed. | Can extract espresso and foam/steam milk simultaneously. Both processes completed within **20-25 seconds total time.** |
| Many home machines must be primed before each use (a separate operation). | Priming not required. |
| Only the better machines have high pressure extraction, 130 P.S.I., required to separate, (emulsify) the oils and colloids from the coffee and produce crema. | High pressurized espresso extraction resulting in crema with each shot of espresso. |

# MACHINE COMPARISON, cont.

| Home Machines | Commercial Machines |
|---|---|
| Low steam volume requiring additional time to foam/steam the milk. | High steam volume allows fast foaming/steaming of the milk. (15 seconds) |
| Only better home machines include commercial-size porta-filters and brew chamber assemblies. | Heavy duty construction. |
| Manual control over the amount of espresso extracted (must switch pour button *On* and *Off*). | Most commercial machines have an automatic extraction portion control for singles and doubles, and will shut off after the desired portion is extracted. |

# ELAPSED TIME COMPARISON
## Preparing a Latte

| Home Machines | Commercial Machines |
|---|---|
| Espresso extraction at 195°F<br>***30 seconds***<br><br>Wait period for boiler to super-heat to 260°F<br>***30 seconds***<br><br>Milk foaming/ steaming time, 45 seconds to 2½ minutes<br>***90 seconds average*** | Espresso extraction and foaming/steaming milk<br>***20-30 seconds*** |
| **Total time to make a Latte with a home machine—**<br><br>***2½ minutes*** | **Total time to make a Latte with a commercial machine—**<br><br>***30 seconds*** |

Places to purchase your home espresso machine: houseware departments of better department stores, kitchen specialty stores, and retail coffee stores.

Warranty centers for home espresso machines are located in most large U.S. cities.

One major difference between home and commercial espresso machines is the elapsed time it takes to foam/steam milk to 140°F. Six ounces of milk foamed/steamed to this temperature can vary, dependent upon the steam volume of the home machine, from 45 seconds to 2½ minutes. A commercial machine will perform this task in 15 seconds.

To speed the milk foaming process, many home espresso machines include a frothing attachment to the steam wand. These attachments inject additional air into the milk to speed the foaming. Trouble is, they often foam (stretch) the milk without providing enough heat to bring the temperature to the recommended 140°F.

Many people making espressos at home solve the milk-heating problem by pre-heating the milk to 90°-110°F in the microwave before foaming it with the frothing attachment. Unlike the steam wand without the frothing attachment, the frothing attachment will permit the user to foam heated milk.

# LAYERING A LATTE

Pour espresso very slowly and steadily through foam.

Foamed milk

Espresso

Steamed milk

In restaurants lattes are often served layered in clear cups. By slowly pouring in the espresso after the hot milk is poured in, the espresso will layer itself between the steamed milk and foam.

*When using flavors, steam syrups with milk.

Chapter 7

# How to Make
# the Perfect Cup

**ESPRESSO: THE PERFECT SHOT** *by Rich Abker*
If you take the time and use a few steadfast rules, you
can perfect the art of making the very best espresso.
After all, this is the first step to creating perfect lattes,
cappuccinos, mochas, Americanos and their many
varieties.

Step 1: Use only freshly roasted coffee especially
blended for espresso (whole bean).

Step 2: Check your grind daily and adjust burr
settings to maintain the correct grind size
(coarseness/fineness). The grind should feel
slightly smaller than sugar granules when
rubbed between thumb and index finger.

Step 3: Use the correct amount of coffee in your
porta-filter, about 7 grams for a single shot
and 14 grams for a double shot.

Step 4: When loading the porta-filter, use a firm
pack and level your coffee to create a
smooth rich crema with optimum
extraction. Rule of thumb is to exert a firm
push of your hand packer while applying a
slight twisting motion to the coffee.

Step 5: The water temperature at the point of extraction (for both group and porta-filter) is crucial to proper extraction. This should be close to 195°F for best results.

Step 6: Water pressure of approximately 130 PSI. is needed from your espresso machine in order to extract only the best in coffee flavor in a speedy and efficient manner.

Step 7: The amount of hot water used for your shot needs to be proportionally correct for the type of pour required. (The amount of coffee remains the same.)

**The Perfect Latte**

1. Use a fresh roasted espresso blend, finely ground just prior to brewing.
2. Measure 7 grams, (or the amount your coffee roaster or machine manufacturer recommends, 6-8 grams).
3. Your porta-filter and container for collecting the extracted espresso should be preheated.
4. Pack the measured grounds into the brew basket; insert into the machine and begin extraction of 18-23 seconds.
5. Pour very cold milk into steam pitcher until it is ⅓ full.
6. Turn on the steam wand for about three seconds, to bleed out any excess moisture that will otherwise dilute your milk.
7. Insert the steam wand in the middle of the pitcher with the tip approximately ½" below the milk's surface. *Turn on the steam wand fully.*
8. Stretch (foam) milk for three to four seconds by lowering the pitcher slightly while listening for a hissing (*sssst-sssst*) sound as the milk takes in air and expands. Keep the tip of the wand ½" below the milk's surface.

9. Now tilt your pitcher about 45°F until a whirlpool action is created. Keep the whirlpool going as you *slowly* lower the pitcher, keeping the tip of the wand ½" below the milk's surface.

10. You will hear a hissing sound *(sssst-sssst)* as the milk takes in air while foaming. **Do not break the milk's surface with the tip of the steam wand.** If you do, large bubbles will suddenly appear, and you will lose your dense foam.

11. When the milk stretches (expands) and reaches the top of the pitcher, tilt the pitcher back to the upright position and *lift* the pitcher so that the tip of the wand is at the bottom of the pitcher. Leave in this position until the milk heats to 140°F.

12. Turn off the steam valve while the wand is still in the pitcher.

13. Remove the pitcher and collapse any large foam bubbles by slapping the pitcher on the counter a few times or by tapping the side of the pitcher several times with a large spoon.

14. Immediately after removing the pitcher, turn the steam valve on again to bleed any milk that might have back-siphoned into the wand. Wipe the wand clean with a damp rag.

15. Pour the espresso into the serving cup.

16. Tilt the serving cup slightly toward you and begin pouring the milk down the front of the cup, moving the pour from one side to the other side in a back-and-forth motion.

17. As the cup fills with this marbleization of foamed/steamed milk and espresso, tilt the cup upright and continue the pour until the mixture rises slightly above the cup's rim.

18. With a typical home espresso machine the foaming/steaming process will take anywhere

from 45 seconds to 2½ minutes, depending on the volume of steam. Commercial machines extract the espresso and foam/steam the milk simultaneously, all within 25 seconds.

### The Perfect Cappuccino

1. It is crucial to prepare the milk before pulling the espresso.
2. Pour fresh, cold milk into steaming pitcher until about ⅓ full.
3. Turn on steam wand for about three seconds to bleed out any excess moisture that may otherwise dilute the milk.
4. Position the steam wand just below the milk's surface, in the middle of the pitcher. Turn on the steam fully.
5. Increase the volume of the milk foam rapidly while maintaining tiny bubbles that will create very dense foam. A slow, gentle lowering of the pitcher should produce a continuous (sssst-sssst) hissing sound.
6. Keep adding air into the steamed milk until the foam rises to the top of the pitcher. When the milk stretches (expands) and reaches the top of the pitcher, tilt the pitcher back to the upright position, and *lift* the pitcher so that the tip of the wand is at the bottom of the pitcher. Leave in this position until the milk heats to 140°F.
7. Now turn off the steam and remove wand from milk.
8. Bang the bottom of the pitcher firmly on the counter several times. This will help to collapse the bubbles and thicken the milk foam. Set the pitcher aside to allow separation of milk and foam.

9.  Wipe the steam wand with a clean damp towel. Then clean out any excess milk by bleeding the steam wand for a few seconds.
10.  Now prepare your espresso and pour into serving cup.
11.  Quickly add only the hot steamed milk until the cup is ¾ full. The milk should pour out easily from *under* the denser foam.
12.  Spoon out the dense milk foam to fill the cup about two inches above the cup rim. Shape foam to form a peak (cap) on the cappuccino.
13.  Dust the "cap" with either powdered chocolate, cinnamon, or nutmeg.

This style cappuccino is known as a "wet" cappuccino because steamed milk is used along with the foam.

A "dry" cappuccino is prepared with straight espresso and dense milk foam but no steamed milk.

### The Perfect Mocha

A mocha is a chocolate latte and is usually topped with whipped cream.

To prepare, first add one ounce thick chocolate syrup to the serving cup, add espresso and stir. Then follow instructions for the perfect latte.

There are two standardized methods of pour:
1.  **Ristretto** (short pour): ¾-1 ounce for a single espresso with pour time of 17 to 20 seconds. This is a very strong, highly concentrated form of true espresso coffee.

Ristrettos are most often used to prepare:
  a. European style (especially Italian) espresso: It has a thick body, taste, and aroma and is served straight or with sugar.
  b. Espresso using milk: lattes, cappuccinos, mochas, and brevés.
  c. Americanos (full strength).
  d. Cold espresso beverages.
2. **Lungo** (long pour): 1½ to 2 ounces of single espresso with pour time of 25 to 30 seconds. This medium strength form of true espresso is used to prepare:
  a. American style straight espresso.
  b. Americanos (mild in strength and taste).

Step 8:   The amount of rich golden crema is an indication of how well you did. The crema must be dense with a golden-brown color. Light brown or white foam indicates the beginning of overextraction.

Step 9:   Serve it hot, and serve it quickly. You've served the perfect shot.

The espresso brew method extracts all that is best from the coffee and nothing more.

 High concentration of flavor and aroma is the greatest distinction between espresso and regular coffee.

 Each cup of espresso is individually made to order from gourmet coffee that is ground just prior to brewing.

 The four components of brewing flavorful espresso are the machine, the grinder, the blend of coffee, and the hand of the operator.

 Because 98% of a straight shot of espresso is water, good water quality is fundamental to a good tasting brew.

 The Northwest, Northeast, and parts of the South generally have the best water quality for brewing espresso.

 Hard water works best for brewing tea and batch-brewed coffee. Soft water is best for brewing espresso.

 Chlorination, excessive hardness, brackishness, alkalinity, and mineral content all can have a negative effect on quality espresso beverages.

If excessive chlorination is a problem, simply let the water stand in a large container for 12 to 24 hours. The chlorination will dissipate—resulting in a much improved espresso brew.

In making espresso, water heated to 195°F (just below boiling) is forced through finely ground coffee under pressure. This captures the greatest amount of flavor.

Lighter roasted coffees generally benefit from a slightly lower brewing temperature, while darker roasted beans require a higher extraction temperature.

Water temperature of less than 192°F produces a distinct sourness in the finished espresso, and the color may be a bit lighter than it should be.

A temperature of over 198°F will burn the coffee oils, creating dark flecks in the crema and producing sharp tasting product (overextraction).

As a rule the amount of soluble solids expressed as a percentage of the total weight of the coffee extracted into the water in the brewing process is: 19% for coffee; 25% for espresso; and 30% for Turkish coffee.

Fruit flavored syrups are best for Italian style sodas and for steamers, while nut flavored Italian style syrups generally taste best in espresso blend beverages.

Darker roasting swells the beans and allows the water more completely to penetrate the finely ground particles during the espresso brewing process. It also reduces the acidity. Filtered coffee can be made from either dark or light roasts, but for the espresso brewing method light roasts are not recommended.

A single shot, or "pull" of espresso in commercial operations, varies from 1 to 1½ ounces. Espresso purists prefer 1 ounce for a most flavorful and aromatic extraction.

After 1¼ ounces of water is extracted through a 7 gram portion of grind, the subsequent extraction starts to turn bitter.

Overextraction occurs when you continue to force hot water through the grind that has already surrendered all its flavor oils.

In brewing coffee or espresso, the longer the bean granules are in contact with the water, the larger the granules should be (the coarser the grind). Due to pressurized extraction in the espresso brew process (18-23 seconds), the granules should be ground finer until they are roughly the consistency of sugar.

The optimum machine pressure for extracting espresso is 130 PSI or 9 atmospheres.

Grinding your beans just prior to brewing is the single most important thing you can do to improve the quality of your espresso.

When not in use, porta-filters should be stored attached to the espresso machine to keep them warm. Coffee grounds placed in a cold porta-filter produce a flat tasting espresso.

Always preheat the shot glass or small stainless steel container that collects the espresso from the machine. Ceramic collection cups should also be preheated. A cold container will "shock" the espresso, and the flavor will be jeopardized.

A 7 gram portion, roughly equivalent to ¼ ounce, is recommended for a single shot ("pull") of espresso.

A tamping tool with a flat base should be used to hand pack the coffee in the brew basket with firm downward pressure and a slight twisting motion.

Many espresso coffee grinders have an attached tamper. Italian baristas will never use this device. They will always use the hand tamper as they press downward with a twisting motion to level the grounds in the basket.

# TAMPING TOOLS & TECHNIQUES

Hand Tamper with flat base

Espresso grounds should be tamped firmly into brew basket with a twisting motion to assure a level pack. This will produce an even extraction.

Dr. Illy says there are over thirty million particles of ground coffee in a seven gram single shot serving.

Coffee brew basket which holds 14 to 16 grams for a double

Porta-filter

# BREW HEAD
# ASSEMBLY

## PORTA-FILTER
## (BREW-BASKET)

Baristas always wipe the edge of the porta-filter with the flat of their hands to remove excess grinds before attaching the unit to the machine. Loose grinds would be abrasive to the rubber gasket in the brew chamber.

---

Once the porta-filter is firmly packed, insert it firmly into the machine.

---

A single "pull" of espresso should take from 18 to 23 seconds. As the liquid extracts, it should appear thick and creamy and a little bit lazy.

---

During the brewing process about 10% of the oils in the ground coffee will separate to form the crema.

---

The crema, a golden-brown foam that covers a perfectly brewed shot of espresso, can only be achieved by a high pressured method of extraction.

---

A thick, rich layer of crema impedes the loss of heat and aroma from the espresso before it is consumed.

---

The crema is formed from microscopic bubbles of coffee gas, oils, and gelatinous colloids. These substances are vectors of the wonderful aroma.

Caution: If you notice a dime-size white area in the midst of your golden brown crema, stop the pour. This area represents caffeine and bitter oils from overextraction.

More water passing through coffee grounds does not make the brew stronger. Excess water weakens the finished beverage, and the last flavors extracted are bitter.

The aroma from crema and espresso is made up of more than 700 chemical components.

Foaming and steaming milk with a steam wand is unique to the espresso business.

The steam wand releases a hot-dry steam at a temperature between 250° and 290°F. This steam method actually alters the proteins of the milk and creates a pleasantly different taste that blends well with espresso.

Soft water steams much better than hard water.

Espresso professionals realized early in the history of the technology that steam collected atop the tank could be used to heat milk as well as to provide pressure for extracting the brew. Soon a valve with a long nozzle was placed into the upper part of the tank for this purpose.

Clip-on dial thermometers that attach to the steaming pitcher are a must for the home espresso maker as well as the professional. Only a few seasoned professional baristas are able to steam the milk to the proper temperature by feeling the heat from the pitcher's surface.

Before steaming milk, open the steam valve to clear the condensed water from the nozzle. After the steaming process, open the line once again to force out any milk that might have been siphoned back into the nozzle when the steam nozzle was last turned off.

To steam and foam the milk, use very cold milk. Also, use a cold stainless steel pitcher for the best results. Warm milk will not foam well.

In the steaming process milk proteins are coagulated, resulting in a thick foam.

The lower the butterfat content of the milk, the better it will foam. Thus when using nonfat milk, stop the foaming (stretching) at 60°F and begin steaming, (heating) to 140°F. When using whole milk, stop the foaming at 100°F and begin steaming.

The two phases of foaming and steaming milk are stretching (foaming) and heating (steaming to the correct temperature of 140°F).

# FOAMING AND STEAMING MILK

1. Begin by filling cold stainless steel pitcher slightly more than ⅓ full of very cold milk.

3. After tip of nozzle is ½" below surface of milk, open steam valve completely and tilt pitcher to one side to create a whirlpool.

4. As milk takes in air, you will hear an intermittent ssst-ssst-ssst sound. Keep lowering pitcher as milk stretches and dense foam is created.

5. After the dense foam has formed, heat the milk mixture to the desired temperature. Turn the steam valve off before removing the wand.

2. When tip of nozzle is ½" below surface of milk, open valve rapidly to completely open position; do not open valve partially.

It is difficult to foam (stretch) whole milk after it reaches 100°F unless a frothing attachment is used. These frothing attachments are generally only available with home-type espresso machines.

Steaming milk is easy, but foaming the milk requires an understanding of the technique and its application.

When preparing to foam and steam the milk, place the nozzle of the steam wand into the center of the pitcher, with the tip of the nozzle ½" below the surface of the milk. Open the steam valve fully.

As the tip of the steam wand takes in air from the surface of the liquid, the milk will expand (stretch), forming dense foam.

Slowly lower the pitcher, keeping the tip of the wand just below the surface of the milk as it continues to expand with foam.

In the foaming and steaming process, you are continuously listening for the intermittent hissing sound "ssst-ssst-ssst." This sound is created from taking in air at the milk's surface. This hissing sound is so important for the skilled barista that the phrase, "A blind person can steam milk, but a deaf person cannot," has been coined.

With a commercial espresso machine the foaming and steaming process should only take from 10 to 15 seconds. Once the foam has stretched to the top of the pitcher, it may be necessary to heat the milk to 140°F. Do this by lifting the pitcher so the tip of the wand goes to the bottom of the pitcher for only a few seconds or until the bottom of the pitcher is too hot to touch.

White milk is best steamed to a temperature of 140°F, while chocolate milk is best steamed to a temperature of 150°F.

If you hear a jet-like howling sound during the foaming and steaming process, the steam wand is too far below the surface of the milk. This sound lets you know you are scalding the milk.

Over-steaming or boiling the milk will result in the lactose, or milk sugar, caramelizing. Many can relate this taste to hot milk that has been scorched atop the stove.

Many commercial espresso operations suffer the effects of high employee turnover and inexperienced or poorly trained baristas. Inept operators routinely burn and scorch milk by leaving the steam nozzle in the pitcher too long.

Leftover milk can be re-steamed if it is immediately refrigerated and if new milk is added to regenerate the protein content that creates the foam.

After steaming the milk, always wipe the steam wand immediately with a damp cloth. Forgetting to do this results in caked-on milk, which can be removed by immersing the wand in a pitcher of water, turning on the steam wand, and allowing the hot water to dissolve and loosen the caked-on milk.

Straight espresso flavor begins to fade rapidly as it cools. The beverage should be mixed and served quickly.

The hot foamed and steamed milk (140°F), when combined with hot espresso (195°F), will hold its temperature even in a paper cup, especially if a domed lid is snapped on. This traveling lid with sipping hole has greatly helped popularize espresso beverages for early morning commuters who enjoy their beverages hot.

There are more than 1,200 chemical components in a single roasted coffee bean. Many of the components give coffee the flavor and aroma we enjoy.

The oils and gasses from the fatty substances in freshly ground coffee, along with the gelatinous colloids, cannot dissolve in water. After a high temperature pressurized extraction, they float to the surface, forming the crema and giving the espresso its incomparable aroma.

The coffeol substances within the coffee bean that flavor the brew constitute only ½ of 1% of the weight of the bean.

Arabica coffee beans are more mild, less bitter, and more aromatic than the Robusta beans. However, the less expensive Robusta beans have more body.

Robusta beans contain a greater quantity of chlorogenic acids. These acids have an upsetting effect on the digestive system if they exceed a certain level.

A professional coffee taster is called a "cupper."

Professional cuppers routinely taste 30 or 40 samples daily.

Before cupping can proceed, coffee must cool to a comfortable temperature. Taste components will be masked if the coffee is too hot.

Cupping flavor has two meanings: One is the total impression of aroma, acidity, and the body; the second meaning is that of specific taste— nutty, spicy, chocolaty, earthy, grassy, and so on.

The strength and the body of espresso are not the same thing. Body is the richness or heaviness of the coffee's underlying taste. Strength is how much coffee actually ends up in the brew

Cuppers sip hard so that the oxygen taken in sprays the coffee throughout the mouth and tongue, giving a full spectrum of the taste.

Cupping or sampling is a daily ritual at most coffee companies. Seven and one-quarter grams of coarsely ground coffee are combined with five ounces of boiling water and stirred. After the water cools to a drinkable temperature, a spoon is pushed through the grounds at the top, "breaking the crust," and the coffee is smelled, slurped, and then spat out.

Professional "cuppers" use a cuspidor to expectorate, thus avoiding the effects of a high caffeine intake and bloating.

The "slurp and spit" method of "cupping" (tasting) coffee was developed in the early 1900s by the Folger's® Coffee Company.

The taste buds on the surface of your tongue will immediately detect the three basic flavors: 1) sweetness; 2) acidity, which should be a snappy quality rather than a heavy sourness; and 3) bitterness, which should be faint unless the beans were over roasted or the brew overextracted.

The human tongue includes over 9,000 taste buds. The life span of a human taste bud is said to be ten days.

The receptors on the tongue that identify the three taste characteristics are located on the tip for sweet, on the sides for acid, and on the back or root of the tongue for bitter taste.

Sweetness is the taste most desired by the general public in regard to the taste of coffee.

Because the tip of the tongue is continually being washed by saliva, sweet taste disappears first.

Human taste buds are reportedly more sensitive at sea level than at higher altitudes.

Most experts agree that the electric recirculating percolator popular into the 1970s made the worst coffee ever. Such percolators continually recirculated and rebrewed the coffee.

Bitter tastes linger in the mouth longest because the receptors that identify this taste at the back of the tongue are less frequently washed with saliva.

According to the coffee cupping guidelines of the SCAA the sensory evaluation includes the six basic coffee characteristics:

| | |
|---|---|
| Fragrance | Nose |
| Aroma | Aftertaste |
| Taste | Body |

Both green and roasted beans are visually examined during the cupping. Samples are continually compared one against the other using these guidelines.

# A CUPPER AT WORK

Two tablespoons of ground coffee are placed in 6 oz of hot water.

Examine the aroma of the grounds.

Break the crust and scoop floating grounds out of a cup. Let remaining grounds settle before tasting.

Take a forceful sip, letting the coffee spray over the tongue, toward the rear of the mouth.

Examine the taste sensations:
-Sweetness
-Faint saltiness
-Acidity
-Bitterness

Expectorate into cup or a spittoon.

Rinse mouth with water.

Begin with another bean type.

A rotating professional cupper's table

*Sweetness is the taste most desired by the general public.

The gelatinous colloids that separate (emulsify) in the espresso brewing process coat the roof of the mouth and the tongue and give the beverage body. They also inhibit the receptors of bitter taste.

Good espresso should be strong but not overly bitter.

The dense body of espresso distinguishes it from regular coffee.

Acidity, contrary to popular opinion, is a pleasing sharpness, a piquant quality that accents flavor. Acidity is characteristic of all high grown Arabica coffees and is a trait which should not be confused with sourness.

Without acidity, espresso would be dull or lifeless.

Some experts say that four fifths of what we perceive as taste is a function of aroma.

The human nose can recognize 4,000 different smells.

The most difficult aspect of coffee tasting is judging the aromas.

Our olfactory system, which gives us our sense of smell, continues to perceive the aromas up to ten minutes after drinking an espresso.

Our sense of smell more than any of our other senses makes our final judgment on coffee.

Coffee—along with beer and peanut butter—is on the national list of the "ten most recognizable odors."

Medical experts state that it is the sense of smell, not taste, that greatly diminishes as we age.

A double-blind taste test is one in which the identity of the product being tested is not disclosed to either the tester or the person being tested to avoid slanting the results.

Even expert tasters have great difficulty telling the difference between regular and decaffeinated coffee.

Coffee served in many restaurants has cooled to 160°F by the time it reaches the table. The addition of milk or cream makes the beverage instantly tepid, devoid of many of its flavor essences.

In many upscale restaurants, lattes are often layered (parfait style) in clear cups. By slowly pouring in the espresso after the foamed and steamed milk is poured in, the espresso will layer itself between the steamed milk and foam. When lattes are served in paper cups at espresso carts and stands, the espresso is almost always poured first.

The entire brewing, foaming, and steaming process is very theatrical, and this personal touch helps the barista merchandise his product.

---

Manhattan and Miami are two cities where espresso is generally consumed straight, as in Italy, without adding steamed milk.

---

Prior to the mid-17th century, no coffee drinker would have dreamed of flavoring his beverage with a dairy product. His preference would have been liquor, sugar, candy, honey, or such spices as cloves, cinnamon, ground cardamom seeds and—in some cases—even mustard.

---

For their lattes, Southern Europeans combine milk and espresso simultaneously into a bowl as a favorite breakfast drink.

---

As people age, many lose their ability to digest milk sugar—all but the northern Europeans. Research shows that most people in this region can go on drinking milk into old age.

---

Italians drink their espresso with sugar; the Germans and the Swiss drink their coffee with equal parts of hot chocolate. The Mexicans like their coffee with cinnamon, the Belgians with chocolate, the French with equal parts of hot milk. Ethiopians add a pinch of salt to their coffee. In the Middle East and Africa, cardamom and spices are added, while Austrians add whipped cream. The Moroccans add peppercorns to their coffee.

**Chapter 8**

# Troubleshooting & Equipment Maintenance

Follow the procedures below to achieve the freshest taste in espresso and to save on replacement parts:

Home espresso machines should be cleaned after each use, and commercial machines should be cleaned daily.

- Use a clean moist towel to clean steam wands, hot water spout and glass gauges. Soak steam wand nozzle.
- Use another towel to wipe down espresso machine, counter area, and grinder.

**Home Espresso Machines—Cleaning Procedures:**
1) Wipe down counter area.
2) Wipe down espresso machine.
3) Wipe down espresso grinder.
4) Remove drip tray and clean well.

Note: Each manufacturer has unique cleaning requirements. Refer to your owner's manual for instructions. The cleaning and maintenance procedures are relatively simple when compared to commercial machines.

## Commercial Machines—Daily Cleaning Procedures:

1) Wipe down counter area.

2) Wipe down espresso machine.

3) Wipe down espresso grinder.

4) Remove drip tray and clean well.

5) Place ½ teaspoon coffee oil remover, such as PuroCaf® into drain tray and backflush with hot water.

6) Check for water leaks around drain hose and drain tray.

7) Remove showerhead screen, screw, and any other parts from group. Place loose items in a metal basket and soak in sink filled with hot water and two tablespoons of coffee detergent. Soak overnight. Scrub with firm brush. Rinse in hot water then cold water.

8) Remove metal filter baskets from hand filters. Use one hand filter with the blank filter (no holes) and place ½ to 1 teaspoon of coffee detergent in filter. Place hand filter into group and back flush by triggering hot water through the group. Back flush should take about 30 seconds. Repeat four or five times until water becomes clear. Do each group.

9) Clean and rinse dump box.

10) Clean plastic hopper and grinder with soft and moist bar towel. Clean doser with a soft brush.

One of the most common reasons for bitter espresso is the failure of the operator to clean the espresso machine properly. Coffee oils will become bitter with age and need to be completely removed by cleaning.

---

The number of wear-and-tear parts can be reduced and the life expectancy of your espresso machine increased by many years if a daily maintenance program is followed.

---

For optimum performance and grind, the burr-wheels of burr-grinders should be replaced after 600 pounds of coffee is ground. Six hundred × 50 servings equals 30,000 single shot servings before burr-wheels should be replaced.

---

Hand filters should be mounted in groups (clean) when not being used. This approach provides a better tasting shot because porta-filters remain hot, and a cold surface tends to shock the espresso and flatten the taste.

---

How do you remove a coffee stain? Rinse in cool water, rub with liquid laundry detergent or paste of laundry detergent and water, then launder.

---

Water impurities and rancid coffee will play havoc with espresso equipment in the absence of routine cleaning and water filtration. One maintenance expert claims that 60% of all the problems with espresso machines are water-related.

Hard water is best for tea and batch-brewed coffee. Soft water is best for espresso.

---

The build-up of limescale is a very common problem without a water filtration system. The more water circulated, the greater the limescale build-up. Commercial espresso machines are more prone to this problem.

---

Limescale results from mineral deposits in hard water that collect and form on the interior of the brew tank and tubing. Water flow, temperature, and taste are all affected.

---

Never attach a packed porta-filter to the brew chamber unless the shot will be extracted immediately. Heat radiated from the chamber will burn the fresh grounds, producing a very off taste in the finished drink.

---

Home espresso machines generally come with user-friendly cleaning instructions. Cleaning and maintenance procedures for these units are relatively simple when compared to commercial machines.

---

Espresso needs to be extracted under pressure. The pump should provide required pressure of about nine atmospheres (130 PSI). This means the pressure is nine times normal atmospheric pressure.

## Troubleshooting Guide for Good Espresso

1. Espresso is flat with very little or no crema:
   + Grind may be too coarse.
   + Use coffee that has been ground just prior to brewing.
   + Let machine warm up a little longer. (Proper temperature needed.)
   + Pack coffee with more pressure.
   + Preheat pouring glasses.
2. Espresso is muddy, watery, and bitter:
   + Select a coarser grind.
   + Place more coffee in porta-filter. Fill to rim before packing.
3. Steam lacks adequate volume:
   + Wand is clogged with milk or sugar crystals. Soak wand nozzle and bleed wand.
4. The porta-filter keeps popping out of the group when extracting:
   + Too much coffee is being placed in filter baskets. Keep coffee just under basket rim before packing.
5. Espresso takes too long to extract and produces dark brown specks:
   + Begin extraction as soon as coffee is placed in the group. Coffee oils will burn if held in the group before extracting.
6. Water leaks from porta-filter or group:
   + Rubber group gasket is worn and needs replacement.
7. Coffee pours out too quickly:
   + Grind is too coarse. Correct fineness to a 20-25 second pour.
8. Coffee pours out too slowly:
   + Grind is too fine. Correct coarseness to a 20-25 second pour.

# GRANITA MACHINE

Liquid mix is poured in top of machine and then frozen into a smooth substance consisting of thousands of tiny ice crystals.

A dual worm screw and auger continuously blends, freezes, and dispenses this refreshing mix.

Granita is typically a Mediterranean product made popular by Sicilians.

Numerous Granita flavors are available.

FROZEN PINA COLADA

FROZEN LATTE

To form a smooth consistent slush base, the mixes should contain about 19% sugar in the recipe.

Chapter 9

# Pronunciation Guide & Glossary

## Pronunciation Guide

| | |
|---|---|
| **Americano** | Ameri-CAH-no |
| **Brevé** | BREV-ay |
| **Cappuccino** | Cap-oo-CHEE-no |
| **Crema** | CREM-uh |
| **Creme de Cacao** | KREHM-de-Ko-KO |
| **Creme de Cassis** | KREHM-deh-kah-SEES |
| **Doppio** | DOPE-eo |
| **Espresso** | Ess-PRESS-o |
| **Espresso con Panna** | Ess-PRESS-o CONE PA-na |
| **Espresso Macchiato** | Ess-PRESS-o MOCK-e-AH-toe |
| **Grandé** | GRAWN-day |
| **Granita** | Gran-E-ta |
| **Latte** | LA-tay |
| **Latte Macchiato** | LA-tay MOCK-e-AH-toe |
| **Latteccino** | La-ta-CHEE-no |
| **Maraschino** | MAH-rah-SKEE-no or MAH-rah-SHEE-no |
| **Mocha** | MO-kah |
| **Orgeat** | OR-zhat |
| **Ristretto** | Ris-TRETTO |

# Glossary

### Acidity

A gentle pucker found in the body of a good cup of coffee or espresso. A moderate amount of acidity—but not too much—adds balance to the flavor of coffee.

### Aftertaste

The lingering taste that clings to your palate after swallowing coffee or espresso.

### Aged Coffees

This term normally applies to green coffee beans that have been aged for several years in proper storage conditions. These green beans do not deteriorate but may improve in flavor.

### Americano

A gourmet cup of coffee, made by pouring one or two shots of espresso over a 6-ounce cup of hot water. The crema from the espresso will float on top.

### Arabica

*Coffea arabica* is the original species of the coffee plant found growing wild in Ethiopia, Africa. Arabica coffee beans are the most sought after in the world due to their intense aromatic flavors. These quality beans are used exclusively by specialty or gourmet coffee roasters.

### Aroma

The delightful bouquet of aromatic gasses released by freshly ground coffee.

## Balance

Refers to coffees that offer just the right balance in flavor, aroma, and body after extraction. Balance is also used to describe a nicely blended coffee.

## Barista

An uncommonly good espresso bartender who understands coffee and the espresso machine's purpose. A barista is an expert at making espresso and a master of a variety of espresso beverages.

## Bitter

This taste is perceived toward the rear of your tongue. A slight bittersweet flavor in dark roasts is appealing to some people.

## Blend

A marriage of two or more coffee bean varieties (Colombia, Panama, Cuba, Kenya, etc.) that when mixed together improves the qualities of taste and aroma.

## Body

The strength and viscosity of the coffee extraction.

## Boiler

The hot water and steam source of an espresso machine. Its purpose is to offer hot water at about 195°F for espresso extraction and steam for heating and frothing milk.

## Brevé

Any milk based espresso beverage where half-and-half is substituted for milk. Brevés can be flavored.

## Brew (Porta-filter) Basket

The filter basket inside your hand filter that allows the espresso to be extracted, while holding back the spent grounds.

## Burnt

Carbonized flavor in coffee beans when they have been over-roasted or very darkly roasted. The taste will be burnt or charcoal like.

## Caffeine

One of the most noticeable compounds present in coffee. Caffeine is known for its abilities to alert the mind, stimulate the body's nervous system, and reduce fatigue or sleepiness. Moderation is the key.

## Cappuccino

An espresso based beverage, topped with equal parts of steamed and foamed milk (wet cappuccino). A dry cappuccino is topped with all foamed milk. The milk is foamed/steamed prior to the espresso extraction, allowing the foam to set, or jell. The foam topping is shaped to form a peak (cap) on the cappuccino. Cappuccinos are usually dusted with nutmeg, cinnamon, or chocolate powder.

## Caramelly

The caramel-like body noted in good espresso crema or a flavor found in some coffee beans.

## Coffeol

The oils in coffee that are both soluble and nonsoluble. The nonsoluble oils are emulsified and become rich crema.

## Crema

In good espresso, crema is considered to be the heart of the espresso extraction. Crema is a dense golden brown foam that covers straight shots of espresso. It is thick with aroma and flavor and is a sign of proper extraction.

## Cupping

A tasting procedure used to determine the qualities of taste and aroma in coffees or a specific coffee. The procedure uses freshly ground coffee or coffees placed in a cup. First aroma is examined. Then hot water—just off the boil—is poured over the coffee. Aroma is checked again. The coffee grounds that remain floating are stirred to the bottom of the cup. Tasting is done next by slurping the coffee toward the rear of the mouth then spitting the coffee out instead of swallowing it. This test is performed often by those in the specialty coffee industry as a means of controlling consistency in coffee blends.

## Decaffeinate

Describes a method used to remove about 97% of the caffeine from whole bean coffees. The Swiss Water Process and the methylchloride solvent process are the two most used methods.

## Demitasse

A small porcelain or stoneware cup that holds two to three ounces of straight espresso.

## Doppio

Double shot of espresso with one measure (shot) of water.

**Doser**

A holding chamber for freshly ground coffee used to measure and dispense the correct amount of coffee into your porta-filter. The doser can be a separate piece of equipment but is normally connected to the front of your espresso grinder.

**Double**

Describes the amount of freshly ground espresso coffee which is dispensed into a double porta-filter. A double contains 14 grams, and a single uses seven grams in a single porta-filter. There are two popular styles of making a double: 1) American Style (double)—Double the amount of hot water is used to extract double the amount of coffee. 2) Italian or European Style (doppio)—This method for a double uses a single amount of hot water over a double amount of coffee.

**Earthiness**

This is a term that normally describes the flavor found in coffees processed in the dry or natural way. *Muddy* is another word for earthiness.

**Espresso**

Proper espresso is made from a special blend of Arabica coffees chosen for intense aromatic flavors and quality of performance during extraction. Espresso uses freshly roasted beans that are finely ground in the correct amount, firmly packed and then extracted under pressure. The end result will be a rich concentration of coffee taste and aroma, topped with a dense golden-brown foam called crema.

**Espresso con Panna**

An espresso topped with a dollop of whipped cream.

## Espresso Romano

A serving of straight espresso with a twist of lemon added.

## Estate Coffees

Normally quality Arabica coffees that are grown by a single owner or company on individual farms. Estate coffees are not mixed with coffees from other plantations.

## Flavor

Describes the tastes and aromas given by the coffee in the mouth. Flavor descriptions can be winey, earthy, chocolaty, fruity, etc.

## Fresh

Freshly roasted coffee maintains its freshness for two to three weeks. It is best stored in whole bean form at room temperature with oxygen and moisture excluded. Coffees preserved for long periods in special packaging are not the equivalent of freshly roasted coffees.

## Grandé

Espresso-milk beverages are usually served in an 8-ounce to-go cup called a short; a 12-ounce cup called a tall; or a grandé 16-ounce cup. A grandé normally uses a minimum of 14 grams of coffee (a double).

## Green Coffee

The processed seeds of the coffee cherry are greenish in appearance and are referred to as green coffee. Unripe coffee cherries are sometimes called green coffee as well.

### Grinder

There are basically three types of grinders used for whole bean coffee: 1) hand mill grinder; 2) electric blade grinder; and 3) burr grinder. The adjustable burr grinder is normally the only style grinder that is used for finely ground espresso.

### Group

The metal brewing chamber on your espresso machine where espresso is extracted from the coffee in the porta-filter.

### Hard bean

A term used to describe Arabica beans. These beans develop denseness due to high altitude pressures during growth.

### High grown

Another term that refers to the Arabica coffee species, normally grown at altitudes greater than 2,000 feet above sea level. In fact, most quality Arabicas are grown beyond 3,000 feet.

### Iced espresso based beverages

Serve in clear plastic or clear glassware. If flavored, the flavoring is added first followed by espresso. When thick syrup is used, stir beverage before adding ice. Fill cup with **cold milk**. Top with whipped cream, if desired.

### Italian cream soda (Cremosa)

Similar to Italian soda except soda water is poured to ½" from the top of the cup. Cup is then filled with approximately two ounces of half-and-half. Italian cream sodas may be topped with whipped cream.

## Italian soda

An iced beverage usually served in a 14- to 16-ounce clear plastic cup. The drink is flavored with two ounces of Italian style syrup or syrups (usually fruit-based) and filled to the top with soda water. The recommended mix ratio is one part syrup to four parts soda water. Italian sodas may be topped with whipped cream.

## Latte

An espresso based beverage created by pouring foamed/steamed milk at 140°F down the side of a cup containing a serving of espresso. The pour allows the milk and espresso to marbleize, forming a very dense mixture and allowing the espresso taste to be experienced with the first sip.

## Latteccino

An espresso based beverage with two parts steamed milk and one part foamed milk—a cross between a cappuccino and a latte.

## Lungo

This is the Italian word for *long* and refers to a long pour of espresso. This extraction usually takes 25 to 30 seconds and is primarily used for straight shots.

## Macchiato

The Italian word for *marked*. There are two types of macchiatos: 1) straight espresso marked with a dollop of warm milk froth; and 2) a steamed milk macchiato (latte or cappuccino) where the steamed milk is marked with an espresso poured slowly over the milk foam at the side of a clear glass. This technique will display a layered effect and is used in restaurants.

**Milds**

> An industry name for quality Arabica beans processed by the wet method. The wet method is a quality process to remove the pulp and skin from the seeds.

**Mocha**

> A chocolate flavored latte with an option of whipped cream for garnish and enjoyment.

**Moka**

> Stove top espresso pot. This appliance is used widely in Europe, especially in Italy. Steam pressure created from hot water in the bottom chamber pushes hot water up a metal tube to extract the espresso in the top chamber.

**Mouth feel**

> The sensation of coffee clinging to the inside of your mouth. Determination of body and degree of aromatics are experienced during mouth feel.

**Nutty**

> Nuttiness is a flavor perceived in freshly roasted coffee similar to that experienced in eating roasted sunflower seeds. Nuttiness is normally considered a good flavor if it is in balance with other aromatic qualities of the coffee.

**Overextraction**

> Caused by the continuous flow of hot water over ground coffee (espresso) even after all of the good qualities have been released. Overextraction is also caused by too fine a grind or hot water temperatures above 197°F, which cause bitterness.

**Peaberry**
> This is a single elongated coffee bean (seed) that can develop in a coffee cherry due to poor pollination during the flower stage. This process happens in only about 2% of the harvested cherries. Peaberries tend to be more flavorful than normal coffee beans.

**Porta-filter (brew-basket)**
> A portable hand filter used to hold coffee during the espresso extraction process. The actual filter basket is removable and is held in place by a single circular spring. Generally there are two types of porta-filters: a single, which has a single spout for the pour and holds between seven and eight grams of finely ground espresso to be extracted in the group brewing chamber; and a double, which has two spouts below the filter basket for the pour. A double basket will hold 14 to 16 grams of coffee. The output can be used to serve one double or two single espressos.

**Pyrolysis**
> The chemical changes occurring during the roasting process. Compounds are developed that will become aroma, taste, and body upon completion.

**Rancidity**
> The tainting and spoiling of the coffee oils, which produce bitterness and a rancid flavor.

**Recovery time**

A term that refers to the amount of time an espresso machine may need to recover either the proper hot water temperature for extraction or the proper temperature to produce steam. Today recovery time is either reduced or eliminated by a) adequate boiler size; b) configuration and size of heating element (proper wattage-to-water ratio); and c) fresh water heat exchangers.

**Richness**

The intensity of aromatic flavors in the body of a good coffee blend, especially prevalent in espresso blends.

**Ristretto**

Ristretto means *restricted* in Italian. It is a short pour of espresso (highly concentrated) using three-quarters to one ounce of hot water to extract the correct amount of coffee in a double or single portion.

**Robusta**

Commercially, the second largest selling species of coffee. *Coffea canephora* was first discovered growing wild in the Congo in Africa. Because Robusta lacks intensity in flavor as compared to the Arabica coffees, it is usually sold as filler coffee for canned blends sold in supermarkets or as instant style coffees. Robustas have twice the caffeine of Arabicas.

**Short**

The size of an espresso to-go cup that will hold eight ounces of any espresso beverage.

## Single

This is a pull of seven grams of freshly ground coffee for espresso extraction. A single (or double) can be extracted as a short pour (ristretto) or a long pour (lungo) for the desired intensity.

## Sourness

A taste associated with coffees picked before ripening or with coffees that are overpoweringly acidic.

## Specialty Coffees

Also known as gourmet coffees or whole bean coffees that have been freshly roasted. These coffees will be quality Arabicas that are sold as a blend from a roaster's recipe or as straight varietals.

## Steam wand

A long metal tube or wand that connects to the top of the boiler to draw pressurized steam. This wand is used for heating and frothing milk as an ingredient in espresso beverages.

## Steamer

A serving of foamed/steamed milk, which has been flavored with one ounce of Italian style syrup. Usually topped with whipped cream. **No espresso** (Same as hot chocolate, but using Italian style syrup for flavoring the milk).

## Tall

A tall refers to a 12-ounce to-go cup, usually filled with steamed milk drinks and espresso or Americanos.

**Tamper**

A tool for firmly packing fresh espresso coffee into the filter basket held by your porta-filter. The best tampers are handheld and offer control of pressure and levelness of packing.

**Under-extraction**

This is one of the most common failures of the extraction process. Proper extraction only occurs when all of the best of the coffee has been removed and offered in the cup. When hot water passes too quickly through the coffee, or when the hot water temperature is below 192°F, some of the goodness remains in the coffee grounds. This failure in technique is called under-extracting.

**Varietal coffees**

These are unblended, straight coffees from a specific country or region. Examples are: Colombian, Costa Rican, Jamaican, Cuban, or Ethiopian coffees. A blend is made when these varietals are mixed.

**Whole bean coffee**

Refers to coffee sold in the whole bean state. Normally, Arabica beans of good quality are sold this way.

**How to Say Coffee Around the World:**

| Country | Language | Coffee |
| --- | --- | --- |
| Cambodia | Khmer | Gafé |
| China | Mandarin | Kafei |
| China, Hong Kong | Cantonese | Kia-fey |
| Czechoslovakia | Czech | Kava |
| Denmark | Danish | Kaffé |
| Egypt | Egyptian | Masbout |
| Eskimo | Eskimo | Kaufee |
| Europe, Israel | Yiddish | Kavé |
| Finland | Finnish | Kahvi |
| France | French | Café |
| Germany | German | Kaffee |
| Greece | Greek | Kafes |
| Hawaii | Hawaiian | Kopé |
| Hungary | Hungarian | Kavé |
| India | Hindi | Coffee |
| Indonesia | Indonesian | Kope |
| Iran | Iranian | Gehvé |
| Iraq, Jordan, Lebanon, Syria | Arabic | Qahwa |
| Israel | Hebrew | Kavah, Kaffee |
| Italy | Italian | Caffé |
| Japan | Japanese | Koohii |
| Laos | Laotian | Kafe |
| Malaysia | Malayan | Kawa, Koppi |
| Mexico, Spain | Spanish | Café |
| Netherlands | Dutch | Koffie |
| Norway | Norwegian | Kaffé |
| Philippines | Tagalog | Kapé |
| Poland | Polish | Kawa |
| Portugal | Portuguese | Café |
| Romania | Rumanian | Cafea |
| Rome | Latin | Coffea |
| Russia | Russian | Kofé |
| Spain | Basque | Kaffia |
| Swahili | Swahili | Kahawa |
| Thailand | Thai | Kafé |
| Turkey | Turkish | Kahvé |

# Works Cited

Armstrong, John. *VIP's All New Bar Guide.* Greenwich, CT: Fawcett Publications, Inc., 1960.

Barbieri, Heather Doran. *Seattle Emergency Espresso.* Bothell, WA: Alaska Northwest Books, 1992.

Baxter, Jacki. *The Coffee Book.* Secaucus, NJ: Chartwell Books Inc., 1985.

Bersten, Ian. *Coffee Floats—Tea Sinks.* Australia: Helian Books, 1993.

Blocker, Lynn. *Bon Appetit Cocktail Parties.* Los Angeles, CA: The Knapp Press, 1983.

Bramah, Edward & Joan. *Coffee Makers.* London: Quiller Press, 1989.

Brandt, Jane. *Drinks Without Liquor.* New York: Workman Publishing, 1983.

Burnam, Tom. *The Dictionary of Misinformation,* New York: Ballantine Books, 1980.

Castle, Timothy James. *The Perfect Cup.* New York: Addison-Wesley Publishing Company, Inc. 1991.

Conran, Terence and Caroline. *The Cook Book.* New York: Crown Publishers, Inc., 1980.

Cooper, Rosalind. *Spirits & Liqueurs.* London: HP Books, 1982.

Cox, Jill. *The Non-Alcoholic Pocket Bartender's Guide.* New York: Simon and Schuster, 1988.

Davids, Kenneth. *Coffee—A Guide to Buying, Brewing & Enjoying.* Santa Rosa, CA: 101 Productions/ The Cole Group, 1991.

Davidson, Alan. *Fruit—A Connoisseur's Guide.* New York: Simon and Schuster, 1991.

Donovan, Jane. *The Miniature Book of Coffee.* New York: Crescent Books, 1991.

Doxat, John. *The Indispensable Drinks Book.* New York: Van Nostrand Reinhold Company, 1981.

Embury, David A. *The Fine Art of Mixing Drinks.* Garden City, NY: Doubleday & Company, Inc., 1958.

Escoffier, A. *The Escoffier Cook Book.* New York: Crown Publishers, Inc., 1969.

Feller, Robyn M. *The Complete Bartender.* New York: Berkley Books, 1990.

Ferguson, William P. *How to Open Your Espresso Cart.* Seattle, WA: Peanut Butter Publishing, 1993.

Ford, Gene. *Ford's Illustrated Guide to Wines, Brews, & Spirits.* Dubuque, Iowa: Wm. C. Brown Publishers, 1983.

Foster, Carol. *Cooking with Coffee.* New York: Simon & Schuster, 1992.

*The Franchise Handbook.* Milwaukee, WI: Enterprise Magazines, Inc., 1993.

Grossman, Harold J. *Grossman's Guide to Wines, Spirits, and Beers.* New York: Charles Scribner's Sons, 1964.

Hattox, Ralph S. *Coffee and Coffeehouses.* Seattle, WA: University Of Washington Press, 1991.

Hoffman, Mark S. *The World Almanac and Book of Facts—1993.* New York: Pharos Books, 1992.

Illy, Francesco and Riccardo. *The Book of Coffee.* Milano: Arnoldo Mondadori Editore S.p.A., 1989.

Jones, Stan. *Jones' Complete Bar Guide.* Los Angeles: Barguide Enterprises, 1977.

Jurich, Nick. *Espresso—From Bean to Cup.* Seattle, WA: Missing Link Press, 1991.

Katona, Cristie and Thomas. *The Coffee Book.* San Leandro, CA: Bristol Publishing Enterprises, Inc., 1992.

Katsigris, Costas & Porter, Mary. *Pouring for Profit.* New York: John Wiley & Sons, 1983.

Kolpas, Norman. *A Cup of Coffee.* New York: Grove Press, 1993.

Lavazza. *Coffee: A Part of Nature's Bounty.* Team Europa.

Louis, David. *2201 Fascinating Facts. U.S.:* The Ridge Press, Inc., 1983.

Mariani, John F.. *The Dictionary of American Food and Drink.* New York: Ticknor & Fields, 1983.

Mariano, Bernard N. *Crema—The Heart and Soul of Italian Espresso.* Chicago: Trendex International, Inc., 1991.

Mario, Thomas. *Playboy's Host & Bar Book.* Secaucus, New Jersey: Castle Books, 1981.

Martin, Kymberly and Dennis. *Recipes for Espresso Magic.* Lake Forest Park, WA: Shady Lane Enterprises, 1991.

McCoy, Elin & Walker, John Frederick. *Coffee and Tea.* New York: New American Library, 1988.

Netzer, Corinne T. *The Complete Book of Food Counts.* New York: Dell Publishing, 1991.

Panati, Charles. *The Browser's Book of Beginnings.* Boston: Houghton Mifflin Company, 1984.

Perry, Sara. *The Complete Coffee Book.* San Francisco: Chronicle Books, 1991.

Poister, John J. *The New American Bartender's Guide.* New York: Penguin Group, 1989.

Regan, Gary. *The Bartender's Bible.* USA: Harper-Collins Publishers.

Roden, Claudia. *Coffee.* London: Penguin Group, 1981.

Rolnick, Harry. *The Complete Book of Coffee.* Militta, 1992.

Rosen, Marcia & Hunt, Gerry. *The Cheers Bartending Guide.* New York: Simon & Schuster, 1983.

Rothstein, Jamie. *Mr. Boston—Official Bartender's Guide.* New York: Warner Books, Inc., 1988.

Schapira, Joel, David, & Karl. *The Book of Coffee & Tea.* New York: St. Martin's Press, 1982.

Schumann, Charles. *Tropical Bar Book.* New York: Stewart, Tabori & Chang, Inc., 1989.

Simmons, Marie & Lagowski, Barbara J. *The Bartender's Guide to Alcohol-Free Drinks.* New York: The Penguin Group, 1990.

Spath, Siegfried. *Driver-Friendly Drinks.* London: W. Foulsham & Co. Ltd., 1990.

Sturdivant, Shea, & Terracin, Steve. *Espresso Drinks, Desserts and More.* Freedom, CA: The Crossing Press, 1991.

Sutton, Caroline. *How Do They Do That?* New York: A Hilltown Book, 1982.

Taylor, Sidney B. *Wine...Wisdom... & Whimsy.* Portland, OR: Winepress Publishing Co., 1969.

Tekulsky, Mathew. *Making Your Own Gourmet Coffee Drinks.* New York: Crown Publishers, Inc., 1993.

Trader Vic. *Trader Vic's Book of Food & Drink*. New York: Gramercy Publishing Company, 1981.

Walker, Michael. *The Cocktail Book*. Tucson, AZ: HP Books, 1980.

Ward, Mary. *The Top 100 Coffee Recipes*. Hollywood, FL: Lifetime Books, 1992.

Williams, Edward E. *The Concise Bar Guide*. New York: Berkley Books, 1990.


## Other Industry and General Reference Works Cited

*Cafe Olé,* Seattle, WA.

CBI. *Coffee & Tea Handbook*. Portland, OR.

Clark, Cynthia J., coffee historian and writer.

*Consumer Reports.*

*Espresso 101 Video*. Media Productions, 1993.

*Fancy Food* . Chicago, IL.

*Fortune.* New York, NY.

*Fresh Cup.* Portland, OR.

*Gourmet Coffee Video*. Auburn, CA: Flessing & Flessing, Walters Productions, 1994.

*Gourmet Retailer.*

*Nation's Restaurant News.* New York.

*The News Tribune.* Tacoma, WA.

*Restaurant News.* Washington, DC.

*Seattle Post Intelligencer.* Seattle, WA.

*Seattle Times.* Seattle, WA.

Starbucks. *Coffee Matters.* Seattle, WA.

*Tea & Coffee Trade Journal.* New York, NY.

*Valley Daily News.* Kent, WA.

*Wall Street Journal.*

*World Coffee & Tea.* Rockville, MD.

During the past few years I have been very fortunate to have been closely associated with Food Equipment Northwest, in Seattle, Washington. I have represented their complete lines of food service equipment which include the Brasilia espresso machines.

Before the formation of Food Equipment Northwest several years ago, the principals, Bill Adams, Glen Coulter, Scott Sensenbrenner, Larry Sandusky, several sales and service representatives, and I were associated while working for another large food equipment company.

Bill, Glen, Scott, and Larry, thank you for your support and your counsel on this research and writing project. You and your network of other food and beverage service experts have continually supplied information and advice to this work. Your examples of customer service, follow-up, and professional ethics have made me proud to be part of your team.

I wish to especially thank Scott Sensenbrenner, sales manager of Food Equipment Northwest, for his patience and supportive guidance of this project.

I highly recommend this company and their national espresso cart sales and service program.

# Index

## A

## B

## H

Haas, Marvin I. 191
Hard bean 274
Harvesting (picking coffee) 133,
    169-171, 174, 175, 180
Hawaii 174, 175, 281
Health departments/regulations
    155
Hemp 179
Hersey, Milton 5
Hersey, PA 5
High grown coffee 172, 258,
    274
Hills Brothers® Coffee 141
Honey 9, 10, 13, 14, 22, 46,
    75, 76, 79, 80, 99, 114,
    117, 136, 205, 260
How to say *coffee* around the
    world 281
Hulling machines, coffee 176
Human nose 258
Humidity 176, 229

## I

Ice 6, 16, 17, 19, 136, 266,
    274
Ice cube 19, 20, 199
Iced coffee 18, 19, 164, 274
Illycaffe® 146
Illy, Dr. Ernesto 146
Illy, Dr. Francisco 146, 214, 245
India 193, 281
Indonesia 174, 281
Indonesian Islands:
    Java 173, 174,
    Sulawesi (Celebes) 174
    Sumatra 174
Instant coffee 145, 149, 169
Irish coffee 144

Italian Cream Soda (Cremosa)
    17, 27, 274. See also
    recipes 30-130.
Italian Soda 17, 19, 26, 154,
    204, 275. See also recipes
    30-130.
Italian style syrups, see Syrups
Italy, Italian 3, 4, 28, 133, 136,
    140, 142, 145, 146, 150,
    163, 181, 184, 208, 214-
    216, 218, 260, 276, 281

## J

Jackson, Andrew 142
Jamaica 149, 173, 280
Jamaican Blue Mountain coffee
    149, 173
Japan, Japanese 18, 149, 156,
    164, 173, 203, 281
Java 172, 173, 198
Jones, Dorothy 136
Jordan, Phyllis 18

## K

Kaldi (goatherder) 132
Kessel 140
King Louis XIV 137
Kola nut 185
Kona, HI 174
Kona Festival 174

## L

Labor 151, 175
Lactase, lactose 4, 159, 163, 206
Latte, drink 4, 8, 12, 15, 16,
    18, 24, 27, 159, 162, 206,
    232, 235, 236, 239, 260,
    267, 275, 276. See also
    recipes 30-130.

Organic coffee 158, 172
Orient 134

## P

Packaging, coffee 140, 141,
146, 164, 190, 273
Paoletti, Sr. 216
Parchment, of green coffee
beans 170
Paris, France 19, 21, 137, 138
Peaberries, coffee beans 171, 277
Penn, William 136
Penny post offices 135
Penny universities 135
Peppercorns 260
Percolation, brewing method
213
Percolator, coffee maker 144,
145, 146, 256
Persia 133
Philadelphia, PA 139, 202
Picking coffee, see Harvesting
Pineapple pulp 149
Pioneer Square, Seattle, WA 18
Porta-filter (brew basket) 192,
216, 220, 225, 229, 231,
235, 236, 244, 245, 246,
247, 263-265, 269, 270,
272, 274, 277, 280
Portions, ingredient 27, 29,
163, 192, 200, 244
Portland, OR 204
Pre-infusion 216
Pregnancy report 148
Priestley, Joseph 198
Processing, coffee 169, 176,
179
Pronunciation guide 267
Proteins, milk 4, 248, 249, 252
Puget Sound, Washington State 4
Pyolysis 183, 277

## R

Recipes: See Chapter 2,
alphabetical listing.
Recovery time, espresso machine
278
Retro® coffee maker 160
Rhode Island, United States 204
Ristretto, drink 9, 14-16, 28,
211, 239, 240, 267, 278,
279. See also recipes 30-
130.
Roasters:
boutique 180
commercial 5, 6, 174, 180,
181, 268
exhibition 159, 160, 169
Roasting, coffee 133, 140, 141,
169, 178, 180-184, 243,
277
Robusta, *Coffea robusta* or
*canephora* 1, 145, 169,
172, 184, 254, 278
Roosevelt, Teddy 142
Rotary pump 216
RSVP International, Whsle.
Coffee Access., Seattle, WA
155

## S

Salt 202, 257, 260
San Francisco, CA 144, 166,
180, 188
Sanka® coffee 142
Sao Paulo, Brazil 150
SCAA 2, 3, 157, 164, 165, 256
Scandinavia 150
Schafer, Charles and Violet 146
Seattle, WA 3, 6-8, 18, 19, 152,
155, 159, 161, 204
Seattle's Monorail 152

Trends, life cycle of 167
Trends Research Center 167
*Trip Through Happy Arabia,*
    book 137
Troubleshooting, espresso
    machines 265
Tupper, Earl W. 191
Tupperware® 191
Turin, Italy 140, 208
Turkey, Turkish 133, 134, 137,
    147, 242, 281
Turkish coffee 134, 242

## U

United States 2, 139-141, 148,
    151-153, 157, 173, 174,
    184, 189, 204, 208, 216,
    218
USDA, milk calorie report 207

## V

Vacuum pack, packaging coffee
    141
Valente, Ernesto 215
Vancouver B.C., Canada 189
Varietal coffees 280
Venice, Italy 133, 136-138
Vibrating pump 215
Voltaire 147

## W

Walgreen's Drug Store 142
Warranty, espresso machines
    225, 233
Washington State 20, 159, 161,
    206

Water:
    chlorination 241, 242
    hard 217, 241, 248, 264
    pressure 215, 236
    quality 241, 263
    soft 241, 248, 264
    temperature 221, 223, 224,
        236, 242, 264, 269, 280
Wattage 217, 225, 278
*WC&T,* magazine 160, 187,
    191
West Coast, United States 186
West Indies 20
Wet season, growing coffee 171
Whipping cream 8, 14, 16, 21,
    24, 26-28, 144, 199, 210,
    211. See also recipes 30-
    130.
Whole bean coffee 2, 4, 157,
    188, 271, 274, 279, 280
Wholesale stores 155
WIB processing method for
    coffee 176
World War II 143, 201, 221

## X

## Y

Yemen 132

## Z

"I was living in a town that was corrupted by a bean, where there was no place to hide from its influence."

from *The Addict*
New York Film Festival entry

**Look for more exciting new titles
from Phil Janssen.**